ARE YOU PSYCHIC?

UNLOCKING THE POWER WITHIN

ARE YOU PSYCHIC?

UNLOCKING THE POWER WITHIN

DR. HANS HOLZER

Avery Publishing Group
Garden City Park, New York

Cover desigers: William Gonzalez and Rudy Shur
In-House Editor: Amy C. Tecklenburg
Printer: Paragon Press, Honesdale, PA

Avery Publishing Group, Inc.
120 Old Broadway
Garden City Park, NY 11040
1–800–548–5757

Library of Congress Cataloging-in-Publication Data

Holzer, Hans,
    Are you psychic? : unlocking the power within / Hans Holzer
      p. cm.
    Includes index.
    ISBN 0-89529-788-4
    1. Parapsychology 2. Psychic ability. I. Title
    BF1031.H664 1997
    133.8—dc21   97-25529
                                                        CIP

Printed in the United States of America.

10   9   8

CONTENTS

INTRODUCTION

A re you psychic? This is not a rhetorical question. It is a very real question that millions of people all over the world ask themselves: Am I psychic, or what?

The fascination with what used to be called the "sixth sense" goes back to the beginning of time and has taken on many disguises. Today, more than ever, psychic ability is a part of daily life for many people. What only ten or fifteen years ago was scoffed at by many no longer has to be hidden. More and more grown men (and far more women) now acknowledge the existence of a faculty in humanity that is not covered in the standard textbooks, although explanations for the psychic gift, how it operates, and where it originates may differ depending on a person's attitude, philosophy, and prejudices.

It is a commonplace of modern life that things that seemed like science fiction only a few short years ago have now become reality. Dick Tracy's wrist telephone was a crude fore-runner of the cellular telephones we take for granted today. Jules Verne's Martian balloon amused his readers at the turn of the century; today we know a great deal about the Red Planet because our instruments have been there. Leonardo da Vinci actually designed a working submarine, but nobody took him seriously at a time when even the steamship had not yet been invented.

We tend to respect inventions of the material kind—machines and devices that promise us a better life. You design it, you get the components, and you build it, and if you've done it right, it will work. We have no problem accepting the electronic transmission of information over huge distances through space, because we understand how the gadgets work. After all, we built them. But when it comes to unusual human faculties that transcend the limits of current human knowledge and ability, we are very cautious. Concepts like extrasensory perception, the psychic—where do these things originate? Can we control them? Are they dangerous?

Parapsychology is the field of study that seeks to identify and understand the effects of the psychic gift, and to try to deduce its system from the results. The "trouble" with the psychic gift is that it does not conform to the rules and laws of empirical science. The phenomena cannot be duplicated at will in the laboratory. Psychic experiences occur randomly and are difficult to categorize.

We know a lot about the ordinary five senses—how they work, which bodily organs are involved, and what biochemical processes make them possible. But with the sixth sense, we know no such things. There is metaphysical talk about a Third Eye, and the various chakras or focal energy points of the body. But finding the actual organ, the seat of psychic power in man, has thus far eluded us.

It is my conviction that psychic talent is simply a natural component of the human personality, an extension of our psychological makeup that somehow can pierce the curtains of time and space. A huge segment of the earth's population has this gift. Indeed, it may well be that being psychic is the norm, and *not* to have developed this gift represents a type of deprivation. In any case, the psychic ability is a positive factor in our personalities, because it supplements our perception and ability to observe immeasurably. It is patently *not* supernatural but perfectly natural, and there are ways to develop and enhance it, and to control it at will.

This book looks at the many different aspects of the psychic, examining and explaining (as far as is currently possible) each in turn. It also offers specific instructions that will help you to explore, and develop, your own personal psychic potential.

1

WHAT EXACTLY IS PSYCHIC ABILITY?

he term extrasensory perception (ESP) was created by the late Dr. Joseph Banks Rhine. Dr. Rhine was a professor and head of the parapsychology laboratory at Duke University, and perhaps the best known of all ESP researchers. He coined the term to describe abilities that seemed to lie outside of the ordinary five senses. Today, we refer to these abilities more often as the psychic.

We all have an extra sense beyond the five normally relied upon, but only a minority of us are aware of it. An even smaller percentage know how to use this sixth sense to good advantage. The problems of acknowledging this faculty have always been many. In the Middle Ages, extrasensory ability was considered tantamount to witchcraft, and the psychically gifted person had to fear for his or her life. As late as the nineteenth century, anything bordering on the occult was considered religious heresy and had to be suppressed, or at least kept quiet.

Then, with the social and economic changes brought about by the industrial revolution, came an overwhelming emphasis on things material, and science was made a new god. This god of tangible evidence leaped into our present century invigorated by new technological discoveries and improvements. Central to the "scientific religion" is the belief that the only things that are real are those that are available to the ordinary five senses. Anything else is not merely questionable but outright fantasy—and fantasy, of course, serves no useful purpose in our mechanized world.

Laboring in this difficult environment, Dr. Rhine developed a new, scientific approach to the phenomenon of the sixth sense. He brought together and formalized many different research approaches in his laboratory at Duke. But even as he offered proof of the existence of the "psi factor" in the human personality—fancy talk for the sixth sense—Dr. Rhine was attacked by exponents of the physical sciences as being a dreamer or worse. Nevertheless, he continued his work; others came to his aid; and new organizations came into being to investigate and, if possible, explain the workings of ESP.

Defining the sixth sense is simple enough. When knowledge of events or facts is gained without the use of the normal five senses—sight, hearing, smell, touch, and taste—or when this knowledge is obtained in apparent disregard of the limitations of time and space, we speak of extrasensory perception. This sixth sense cannot be turned on at will, but functions best when there is some kind of emergency and there is a genuine need for it. Apparently, when ordinary communications and perception fail, something within us can reach out and remove the barriers of time and space to allow for communication and perception beyond the five senses.

THE PSYCHIC EXPERIENCE

The nature of the psychic is spontaneous and unexpected. You never know if or when you will have an experience, and you cannot make it happen. These experiences are made possible by conditions beyond your conscious knowledge, and you have no control over them. It is possible to learn the art of proper thinking—training yourself toward a wider use of your inherent psychic powers—as we shall see in later chapters. But psychic events themselves are definitely not under your control—or anyone else's, for that matter.

The psychic experience can take the form of a hunch, an uncanny feeling, or an intuitive impression, or it can be stronger and more definite, such as a sudden flash of instantaneous knowledge, an image or auditory signal, a warning voice, or a vision, depending on your own makeup and inborn talents as a receiver. I also refer to the substance of a psychic message as *cognizance*, since it represents instant knowledge obtained without any "logical" basis or process.

When confronted with a psychic message, most people's first impulse is to suppress it or to explain it away. Sometimes people go to great lengths to avoid admitting the possibility of extrasensory experiences. This can lead to tragedy or, at the very least, to annoyance; for the psychic impulse is never in vain. It may be a warning of disaster or advance notice of an opportunity ahead, but it is always significant, even if you miss the meaning at the time or choose to ignore it.

Dr. Louisa Rhine, wife of Joseph Rhine and a biologist in her own right, had this to say about the psychic and its relationship to the human mind:

> Just what the mind is and exactly how it operates are still deep mysteries to science. But at least some explanation can be made by assuming the existence of a still largely unrecognized mental ability, to which the term "psi" has been applied.
>
> Telepathy (the communication of thoughts from mind to mind) and clairvoyance (seeing events before they happen), both manifestations of psi, have come to be recognized as two of the main types of extrasensory perception. Both are ways of getting information about the world. In telepathy, the information comes from other people's thoughts; in clairvoyance, it comes from events or objects. A third type of ESP, by which information comes from events that have not yet taken place— in other words, the ability to look into the future—is known as "precognition." Most psi phenomena can be accounted for by one of these three, or possibly by a combination.
>
> There is no way of being sure. In fact, . . . there may be no fundamental difference between the processes of telepathy and clairvoyance, except for one having a subjective origin (thoughts) and the other an objective one (things and events).
>
> Whatever the exact nature of psi, it seems to be unaffected by distance, functioning just as easily whether the persons, objects, or events are separated by a room, town, continent, or ocean. And in the case of precognition, we see that psi, even more incredibly, is apparently also independent of time.

As a sixth sense, ESP is really far more than an extra sense, equal in status to the other five. It is actually a *supersense* that operates through the other five to get messages across to human consciousness. A sixth-sense experience may come through the sense of sight—as a vision, a flash of knowledge, or an impression; the sense of hearing—as a voice or a sound effect duplicating an event to be; the sense of smell—as a strange scent associated with another climate, or with certain people or places; the sense of touch—the feeling of a hand on the shoulder, a furtive kiss, or a sense of being touched by unseen hands; and/or the sense of taste—stimulation of the palate not caused by actual food or drink. Of the five ordinary senses, by far the majority of psychic experiences involve either sight or sound or both. The senses of smell, taste, and touch are rarely involved. I believe this is because the senses of sight and hearing are the ones most responsible for informing the conscious mind of the world around us.

DEMONSTRATING THE EXISTENCE OF THE PSYCHIC

Because extrasensory phenomena are governed by emotional impulses, research into the psychic presents certain problems. There have been successful experiments using cards, dice, and other tools to detect psychic ability, but spontaneous psychic experiences cannot be duplicated at will. Parapsychology—the field of science that investigates phenomena of this kind—has frequently been attacked on these grounds. We should remember, however, that researchers in the fields of psychology and psychiatry, which also deal with human emotions, cannot duplicate phenomena in the laboratory, either. These sciences were once attacked much as parapsychology is today, and only relatively recently have they found a comfortable niche of respectability. Fifty years from now, parapsychology will no doubt be one of the older sciences, and hence accepted.

If it is to be meaningful and valuable, psychic perception research must involve spontaneously arising cases in the field—that is, real-life psychic experiences. It does not rely entirely on such cases, but without them it would be meaningless. Laboratory experiments are an important adjunct, particularly when we are dealing with less complicated phenomena such as telepathy, intuition, and psychic concentration, but they do not have the same impact as cases of genuine precognition (foreseeing events before they occur) and other one-time events in human experience. In this, parapsychology is no different from certain of the physical sciences. In fact, some of the natural sciences could not exist if it were not for field observations. Just try to reconstruct an earthquake in the lab, or a collision of galaxies, or the birth of a new island in the ocean!

The critical things, of course, are, first, ensuring the presence of competent observers and, second, learning the frequency with which similar, but unrelated, events occur. For example, if a hundred cases involving a poltergeist (a "noisy ghost") are reported from widely scattered areas, involving credible witnesses who could not possibly know of each other or have communicated with each other, or have had access to information about the events they report on, it is perfectly proper scientific procedure to accept the reports as genuine and to draw certain conclusions from them.

I take a middle-of-the-road approach to the subject of the psychic, being neither credulous or incredulous. The will to *dis*believe is, in my opinion, the strongest impediment to broadening our horizons. The will to discount that which does not conform to inbred beliefs and conventions is a sign of our materialistic age, in which individual impulses are discouraged in favor of "belonging" to groups that are scientifically or socially acceptable (preferably both). What is left behind is, of course, the one thing humankind needs if it is to avoid dying by its own hands: *progress.*

WHAT KIND OF PEOPLE
ARE INTERESTED IN THE PSYCHIC?

The notion still persists among large segments of the population that the psychic is a subject suitable only for certain people—the weird fringe, some far-out scientists, perhaps, or young people who are "into the occult." Under no circumstances would it be something for respectable, average citizens to get involved with. This attitude is generally more pronounced in small towns than in large, sophisticated cities, but until recently, at least, the notion that the psychic might be a subject for average people or broad-based interest was alien to the public mind.

In recent years, however, this attitude has shifted remarkably. More and more, discussions of extrasensory perception and related subjects are welcome in many social circles, and those with knowledge of them become centers of attention. Especially among the young, bringing up the subject of the psychic almost guarantees immediate interest.

Indeed, with ever-expanding communications through television, video, computers, and film, the paranormal, which implies and involves psychic ability, has become quite a "hot" topic. There are a number of popular television programs, both network and cable, that deal with the subject, with varying results. Some present dramatizations of actual cases of psychic phenomena and present the real people involved at the end of the show. These attract fairly large audiences, but, unfortunately, they also tend to take liberties with the material. The label "based on a true story" allows plenty of leeway for upgrading the dramatic content at the expense of the truth. Pure interview or discussion programs, which keep more closely to the facts, have fared badly; most viewers want something more visual, more exciting to watch.

To the average person not involved in the study of psychic experiences, apparently, there is little difference between fiction that touches on the subject of the paranormal and the real thing. Still, the growing interest in the paranormal does indicate a greater general awareness of the existence of the psychic, and that is to be welcomed.

True, some people—especially those in business or government—will raise an eyebrow when the psychic is mentioned as a serious subject. You still occasionally hear the comment, "You don't really believe in that stuff—?" Occasionally, too, people will argue with you, saying that all psychic phenomena are fraudulent and have "long been proved to be without substance." (It is remarkable how some of those avid scoffers quote "authoritative" sources that they never identify by name or place.) Of course, people will believe what they want to believe. If a concept makes you uncomfortable, you will find reasons not to believe it, even if you have to drag them in out of left field.

The types of people who are interested in the psychic include some very strange bedfellows. On the one hand, there are increasing numbers of scientists delving into the area with newly designed tools and new methods; on the other hand, there are laypeople in various fields who find the psychic a fascinating subject and do not hesitate to admit their interest in it. I know from experience that it is intensely interesting to all kinds of people who would not have thought of it a few years ago—among them university professors, doctors (even psychiatrists), investment bankers, police officers, military service members, and others. I have talked with hundreds of people in all walks of life, in the United States and abroad, and I have found that many have had firsthand experiences and therefore accept the psychic as real. I have also met people who have not had psychic experiences themselves, but who know people who have and do not doubt them; they know these witnesses well enough to judge their reliability.

Then, too, I have found people—often people with important and/or public positions—who in private admit candidly that they have had proof of the existence of the psychic, but who will not say so in public or for the record. For example, one well-known actor told me about experiences he had had with old-time spiritualists; he said he had attempted to find evidence that the phenomena he observed might have been fraudulently manipulated, and he failed. But he was less forthcoming about this when I interviewed him for my radio series. Another noted actor told me that he had seen a plane crash before it occurred, and described it to his wife just in time for both of them to take shelter—but I could not get him to repeat the incident for publication. A New York politician who owned a house on Nantucket told me that he and his wife had both heard footsteps coming up the stairs when no one was there. But to say so publicly might ruin his chance for political office. Ghosts, indeed! There were enough skeletons in his closet as it was.

Perhaps not surprisingly, the number of people who accept the existence of extrasensory perception appears to be much larger than the number of people who believe in spirit survival, reincarnation, the existence of ghosts, or other more complicated forms of the paranormal. ESP has something of the scientific about it, while, to the average mind at least, other types of phenomena require the acceptance of something other than the purely scientific.

To accept ESP, one need not accept the survival of the human personality beyond bodily death or anything of that nature—merely an as-yet-unexplained exchange of psychic energy between two people. With ESP, you need only extend the limits of believability a little, not change your framework of belief altogether—at least, that is the widely held conviction. The same cannot be said about the acceptance of spirit communication, reincarnation, and other paranormal phenomena. Accepting these as realities would require a profound alteration in fundamental philosophy, at least for most people.

WHO ARE THE PSYCHIC?

It is my firm conviction that *everyone* has some psychic ability, at least potentially, although most of us do not know it and may not even want to. But some people are fortunate enough to recognize this gift for what it is, accept it, and even use it for their own benefit and for the benefit of others.

Psychic ability is not a supernatural or mystical thing, as many believe; it is simply part of human nature. Of course, as with any human ability, some people have greater natural gifts than others, but we all have capacities that we can learn to use to their fullest extent. People with psychic ability include individuals of every ethnic and religious background, every walk of life, both sexes, and all ages.

It has been observed, however, that certain physical conditions can have an impact on the presence or absence of psychic capabilities. For example, although it is not known why or how this happens, certain accidents can sharply increase a person's extrasensory perception, especially accidents involving head injuries. There was a Dutch psychic named Peter Hurkos some years ago who was an ordinary house painter until he accidentally fell off a ladder and hit his head. After this shakeup, he began to predict future events with great accuracy.

There are also certain groups of people who seem to be likelier than most to have psychic talents. Some of the most interesting cases involve identical twins. Twins often know of each other's whereabouts intuitively; they tend to go through similar experiences even though widely separated in terms of distance; and they frequently feel the same way about individual causes or people. This should not really be surprising. Identical twins—that is to say, siblings of the same sex, resulting from the division of one fertilized egg, and born only minutes or even seconds apart—are connected on a psychical level even though their physical bodies move apart from each other freely. Indeed, the evidence suggests that identical twins in some way maintain a continuing and close psychic communication with each other.

Marlene Rouse of California always thought of her twin sister as her other half, or part of her divided at birth. As a child, Marlene was always the sick one, but her sister always complained of the same symptoms. When Marlene had a ruptured appendix, for example, she and her sister argued over who was the sickest. When Marlene first became pregnant, she learned of it because her sister called to say she had morning sickness; her sister also suffered through Marlene's labor pains with her.

Early one morning, Marlene awoke with pains in her chest and arms. As a former student nurse, she knew the symptoms of a heart attack, and went immediately to the emergency room. The doctor found nothing wrong, but while he was examining her, the symptoms returned. The doctor turned white and rushed out to do an EKG. The results were normal, and the doctor concluded she was faking her symptoms. It turned out that it was Marlene's sister who had heart trouble, and she died of a heart attack within the year.

As a child, Frank Farnsworth and his twin brother Francis lived with their family in rural upstate New York. Late one afternoon, Francis went to an aunt and uncle's house, some twenty miles away, to have dinner. After Francis left, Frank wandered off into the woods and got lost. It became dark, and the boy was frightened. At the same time, Francis was sitting down to dinner at the uncle's house, and he began to cry. When he was asked what was wrong, he said, "Something is wrong with Frank."

The latter case raises also the question of psychic ability in children. I find that children, especially before the age of four or five, are quite often psychic, and can describe situations or scenes or give the names of people they could not possibly know through ordinary means. There have also been cases in which young children have spoken in the voices of adults, reporting in great and authentic detail experiences they could not possibly have had.

Some of what appears to be psychic ability on the part of children may actually be due to reincarnation memories that later fade. There seems to be a period between ages five and eight when such occurrences recede, only to return after the age of puberty. In other cases, children seem to have the same types of psychic gifts that adults do, whether that involves telepathy, clairvoyance, out-of-body travel, psychic healing, or other abilities.

L.J., a young boy, would not go to sleep one night, but instead demanded that his mother come to his bedside. He had something to tell her. "This house is crooked. It's going to fall down," he said. His mother tried to assure him that God would look after them all, and he finally went off to sleep. However, the statement caused L.J.'s mother to remember that when they moved into the house, they noticed that the hardwood floor in the living-room closet did not meet the wall. It had not occurred to her then that this could mean the house was indeed crooked. A week later, the boy still spoke of the house falling down, and asked God not to let it fall on him. He also put his arms around a tree in front of the house, then told his mother, "That tree is going to fall down, too." L.J.'s mother subsequently learned that the house was built over an active earthquake fault.

There is nothing particularly frightening about psychic abilities in children, provided it is handled sensibly by the parents. They should neither deny the fact that their child has had an unusual experience nor particularly encourage the child to dwell on it. Rather, they should point out that ESP is a perfectly natural ability, and gently encourage their child to talk about it with them, as with any other facet of the child's life.

CONVENTIONAL SCIENCE AND THE PSYCHIC

Sometimes a well-meaning but otherwise unfamiliar person will ask me, "How does science feel about ESP?" That is a little like asking how mathematics teachers feel about Albert Einstein. ESP is *part* of science. Some scientists may indeed have doubts about its validity or its potential. However, scientists in one area frequently doubt scientists in other areas. For example, some chemists doubt what pharmacologists say about the efficacy of certain drugs; some underwater explorers differ with the opinions expressed by space explorers. For that matter, some medical doctors disagree with what other medical doctors believe.

Some scientists, trained in traditional if up-to-date ways, consider anything they have not been taught by other establishment scientists to be "unscientific." This is part academic arrogance, part fear of the unknown, and part nineteenth-century materialism. But didn't the top scientists of the time tell Thomas Edison that his incandescent light bulb would never work? And didn't Edison, in turn, tell Alexander Graham Bell that the telephone was nothing more than a novelty, and would never have any widespread practical use?

A definition of science is in order here. Contrary to what some people think, science is not the same thing as knowledge. In fact, it is not even comparable. Science is merely the process of gathering knowledge by reliable and recognized means. These means, however, may change as time goes on, and the means considered reliable in the past may fail the test in the future; conversely, methods not used in the past may come into prominence and be found useful in the future. To consider the edifice of science an immovable object—a wall against which you may lean with confidence that nearly everything worth knowing is already known—is most unrealistic. Just as living things change from day to day, so do science and that which makes up scientific evidence.

The word *science* derives from the Latin verb *scire,* meaning "to know." *Scientia,* the Latin noun upon which our English term *science* is based, is best translated as "the ability to know," or perhaps as "understanding." Knowledge as an absolute is another matter. I doubt very much that absolute knowledge is possible within the confines of human comprehension. What we are dealing with in science is a method of reaching out toward absolute knowledge, not attaining it.

By and large, scientists not directly concerned with the field of parapsychology do not venture into it, either pro or con. They are usually much too concerned with their own fields. Occasionally, people in areas that are peripheral to parapsychology will venture into it—some because they are attracted by it and sense a growing importance in the study of those areas, others because attacking the findings of parapsychology allows them to feel psychologically validated in some way.

Some of the most vociferous and aggressive attackers of parapsychology have included establishment-trained scientists such as psychiatrists, psychologists, and medical doctors, as well as professional magicians and clergy members. Generally, these individuals feel upset, even threatened, by the notion that there may be another order beyond and outside the conventional three-dimensional universe they are familiar with. After all, if there is another order—a world beyond, a paranormal system, and genuine psychic abilities—they would have to reorient their own value systems, even their most fundamental philosophies, and they are not about to do that.

When Joseph Rhine first started his work measuring what he called the "psi" force, it was the first time that an area formerly left to occultists was explored by a trained scientist in the modern sense of the term. Even so, almost no one took the field of parapsychology very seriously. Rhine and his closest associate, Dr. Hornell Hart, were considered part of the sociology department at Duke University, where they worked; there was not as yet a distinct department of parapsychology or a degree in that new science. But the picture is changing. Today, even many orthodox scientists are willing to listen to the evidence for the existence of parapsychological phenomena, and there is a greater willingness to evaluate the evidence fairly and without prejudice.

It is not surprising that some more liberally inclined and enlightened scientists are coming around to thinking that there is something in the psychic after all. Continuing developments and theories in the field of physics may be one reason for this. As far back as 1957, a *Life* magazine editorial pointed out that "[the] basic assumption . . . that the only 'reality' is that which occupies space and has a mass . . . is irrelevant to an age that has proved that matter is interchangeable with energy. . . . [M]etaphysics could well become man's chief preoccupation of the next century and may even yield a world-wide consensus on the nature of life and the universe."

Happily, science is no longer quite as hostile as it used to be to serious inquiry into psychic phenomena, and the renewed interest in things paranormal appears to be genuine. More and more people are curious about this elusive "sixth sense" we all possess. The pioneers in psychic research are all gone now, but a new generation of serious researchers has emerged who are no longer afraid of calling the study of extrasensory perception part of scientific inquiry. They recognize that there is nothing in our world that is not natural, even if we have not yet fully understood it or how it works.

WHY STUDY THE PSYCHIC?

One thing that has struck me, after investigating extrasensory phenomena for twenty-odd years, is the thought that with ESP, we are not really dealing with an additional sense like touch or smell, but with a sense that is nonphysical. Physical reality, in order to make itself known, must go through the physical senses. But what we really have here is an extension of the ordinary five senses into an area where logical thinking is absent and other laws govern.

Proponents of the physical sciences want us to accept the existence of only those things that are readily accessible to the five senses in ways that can be demonstrated in laboratories. By the same yardstick, the existence of radio waves was once judged fantastic. Yet today we routinely use radio to communicate with one another and even to contact distant heavenly bodies. Or we might compare psychic phenomena to the part of the spectrum that is invisible to the naked eye. Infrared and ultraviolet light are extensions of ordinary red and violet light and, although we cannot see them, we nevertheless make use of them and no one doubts that they exist.

It all adds up to this: Our normal human perception, even with instruments extending it a little, is far from complete. To assert that there is no more around us than the little we can measure is preposterous. It is also dangerous, for in teaching this doctrine, we prevent ourselves from allowing our potential psychic abilities to develop unhampered. In a field where thought is a force to be reckoned with, false thinking can be destructive.

THE PSYCHIC VERSUS THE OCCULT

As legitimate research into psychic phenomenon has gained some acceptance in the scientific community, a cleavage between the occult—that is, a mystical, emotional approach to psychic phenomena—and parapsychology—a scientific, clinically oriented approach to these same phenomena—has gradually become apparent. This is not to say that both will not eventually merge into a single quest for truth, but it seems to me very necessary, at a time when so many people are becoming acquainted with the occult, to make it clear that there is a definite distinction between the professor of parapsychology and the tearoom reader.

If you are sincerely seeking information in this field, you should always question the credentials of those who give you answers. In general, researchers with academic credentials or affiliations are more likely to be trustworthy than those who offer only vague platitudes or "doctorate degrees" fresh from the printing press. Lastly, psychic readers who purport to be great prophets must be judged on the basis of their accomplishments in each individual case, not on their self-proclaimed reputations.

With all that in mind, and with due caution, it is heartwarming to find so many sincere and serious people dedicating themselves to the field of parapsychology and scientific inquiry into what is one of the most intriguing and important areas of human endeavor. In the chapters that follow, we shall examine the psychic in all of its many fascinating aspects.

2

TELEPATHY, AND HOW IT WORKS

"It must be telepathy," the astonished person exclaims when someone has just "read his mind." Often erroneously called "mental telepathy," telepathy is communication from mind to mind without making use of the ordinary five senses. The transfer of thoughts from one mind to another is accomplished at great speed. A tiny fraction of time does elapse between the transmission of a thought or image by one mind and its reception by another, but it is so insignificantly small that, for all practical purposes, we can say that telepathy is the instantaneous transmission of thoughts from one person to another.

Strictly speaking, the word *telepathy*, taken from the Greek, merely means "impression across a distance." To the parapsychologist, it represents the simplest and most straightforward form of extrasensory perception. Another name sometimes given this faculty is "thought transference."

THE NATURE OF THOUGHT

A thought is an image or set of conditions created in the mind. It may be generated by the mind itself, or it may be the product of taking note of what you perceive through your five ordinary senses.

A thought is also an electrical impulse that can be sent out by the brain. Since they are electrical entities, thoughts must naturally have some substance, no matter how small. It should therefore be possible to register or measure them, or trace their existence in some other objective way. And, in fact, orthodox medicine has long been measuring "brain waves" by means of the electroencephalograph, an apparatus capable of registering, through electrodes attached to the head, the tiny currents within a person's brain.

Thought waves originate in the mind, which uses the brain as its switchboard. The electricity required to make the process possible is derived from the network of nerve fibers within the human body, which provides sufficient voltage for this. More research is needed to explore the mechanics of thought transmission, but in its basic concept, it is no different from radio transmission, except that it takes place on an infinitely finer and more sensitive scale.

While the mind operates through the brain, the two are not identical. Some scientists still refer to the brain as the seat of thought creation, but it assuredly is not. The brain is merely the transformer, the switchboard, and the storehouse of thought impulses, those sent out and those received. It is the mind that operates and controls the brain; the mind is the real place of origin for the thought process.

THE TELEPATHIC PROCESS: SENDING

When you have an idea, an electrical impulse—a thought wave—is created. Once created, it is sent out by the brain. Ordinarily, people cannot control either the direction or the intensity of these broadcasts. However, gifted individuals can be trained to use thought messages in such a way that they are picked up by a particular receiver on the other end of an invisible "line." If a person who receives a message this way has no foreknowledge of its contents, nor any access to the information contained in it, and the material checks out as true, then we have a clear-cut case of successful telepathy.

Since thought waves, like other types of radiation, give off tiny particles of themselves as they travel along, they gradually become weaker as they radiate outward from the sender.

However, this loss of energy potential is so small that, for all practical purposes, thought waves can travel great distances without apparent loss of clarity. Thought waves do not respect solid objects or other hindrances, either. Thus, we have a type of communication that totally disregards the usual laws of space and time.

A traveling thought wave can pass through walls and, in some way not yet fully understood, be caught or attracted by "tuned-in" receivers. It may be caught by more than one receiver; it may be caught by none. Once a thought wave has been created and is on its way, the sender has no further contact with it. Meanwhile, it continues to travel in every direction until its energy has thinned out to such an extent that it is no longer capable of being received.

If, however, a thought is created and directed specifically at another mind, with the desire that the other person receive it, the thought is usually much stronger and less likely to stray all over the map. And if the intended receiver is attuned—that is, emotionally fit to receive—then thought transfer will take place directly. This may be successful even if the receiver is asleep and the thought reaches his or her unconscious mind. The discipline of the sender is most important. Such thought discipline can be attained by proper training and by proper attitudes.

In general, telepathy seems to work best with thoughts that are conceived spontaneously. For instance, it suddenly occurs to you that it would nice be to see your mother. Your mother lives 500 miles away. Just at that instant, she suddenly thinks of you, and how nice it would be to see you. Coincidence? Not when it happens in thousands of similar cases, many of them easy to verify.

THE TELEPATHIC PROCESS: RECEIVING

Although telepathic messages originate in the mind and are sent out via the brain, they are received on the other end through the unconscious (or, if you prefer, subconscious) part of the mind. With trained experimenters, the conscious part of the mind also can be used to serve as receiver on occasion, but the vast majority of telepathic cases involve spontaneous reception that employs the unconscious part of the mind as its gateway. This eliminates the possibility that such factors as rationalization and rejection might come into play and destroy the message before it is properly evaluated.

The shadings of telepathic communication are many. They run the gamut from vague feelings about distant people or events to clear-cut, sharp, and definite messages instantly capable of verification. It depends on both the sender and the receiver—their individual abilities to free themselves from factors that might inhibit the process, their surroundings, their prejudices, their fears, and the nature or urgency of the message itself. Since comparatively few people understand the workings of telepathy, the average person who has the experience of receiving a message in this way is likely to explain the thought that arises in him or her—and that may prompt action of one kind or another—as a hunch or a sudden inspiration.

The stronger the need, and the greater the emergency, the more likely it is that there will be strong reception. Trifling bits of information are less likely to create remarkable impressions on the other end of the line. There have been cases in which one sender has reached several members of the same family to let them know of an emergency. There have also been cases in which the message was nothing more exciting than a friendly hello from a distance. Telepathy has no hard and fast rules. But it works.

TYPES OF TELEPATHIC EXPERIENCES

As we have seen, telepathy works a little like radio: small impulses, programmed by the sender, are sent out to a known receiver; the receiver, in turn, decodes the message and allows his or her conscious mind to formulate it into words. Telepathy works best between people who know each other, and even better between people who are emotionally close to each other. This is no more astounding than the fact that an electrical plug fits best into a socket especially made for it, or that a stage director likes to work with actors he knows because they can communicate better with each other. A sender and receiver tuned in to one another naturally yield better results than a random beam that is looking for a receiver and losing its energy while searching a very large field.

As we know, all extrasensory experiences are emotionally tinged in that they involve the whole personality. The emotions in question need not be love or hatred. For example, creative excitement is an equally strong emotional force. Many ideas seem to have been "in the air" only to be picked up simultaneously by a number of people quite independently from one another. The same inventions are created simultaneously in widely separated places; pieces of music are written by people who do not know of each other and yet duplicate each other's work.

The world is full of this kind of "coincidence." Some philosophers would have us believe that there is a "world mind," a source from which all knowledge comes—a sort of a super public domain ready to be tapped by anyone with the right tools. But it may be just that one mind gives out strong thought waves, while another, at a distance, receives them, without realizing that the "new" idea really originated in someone else's mind—a kind of innocent plagiarism.

Spontaneous Urgency Telepathy

Telepathy works best in times of stress and when ordinary lines of communication are down. It is particularly strong between people who have an emotional bond, such as relatives, friends, lovers, or people who in some fashion rely on each other. For example, instances in which a mother has felt the distress of a child (at a distance, of course) are quite numerous; there are also many cases attested to in the files of reputable parapsychological research societies in which someone just *had* to get through to another person and used his or her mind to send forth a message.

When ordinary communication is impossible and the initiator of the telepathic message realizes this, forces are brought into play that make the message very strong. The substance of the message may concern a real crisis or a comparatively unimportant matter, but as long as there is an element of urgency *for the person concerned*, and he or she realizes that there is no other avenue to get through, telepathy may indeed succeed. Consider the following examples:

One Saturday afternoon, my wife had gone to see her doctor and I was home alone working. Suddenly I realized my wife would be passing near a specialty shop that sold a certain type of cheese I liked very much. I could not disturb her while she was at the doctor's for an examination, and I knew that she would leave immediately upon its completion. The best I could hope for was that she would telephone me. I did not concentrate on this, but merely held in the back of my mind the thought of her calling me on her own. I knew that she would be at the doctor's at four o'clock. At one minute after four the telephone rang. It was my wife, saying, "You want me to get some cheese, don't you?"

Marlene Rouse, the young California woman mentioned in Chapter 1, learned that her grandfather had died while her mother was away in the gaming resort town of Lake Tahoe. Her mother had not told Marlene where she was staying, so Marlene called every casino she could think of and had her mother paged, with no results. At about eight o'clock in the evening, she gave up. In tears, she closed her eyes, saying, "Mom, where are you?" All of a sudden, the word "blackjack" came into her mind, and she immediately thought, "Oh, no. She's winning. That means she won't come home for at least a couple of days." For about fifteen minutes, Marlene repeated over and over, "Mom, please lose so you'll come home." Then, feeling exhausted, she gave up.

During the night, her mother called, saying that she was staying at a hotel called the Blackjack, and that she had indeed been playing blackjack—and winning—when all of a sudden, between eight and eight-fifteen p.m., she started losing every single hand. Unable to believe that her luck had turned so badly, she went back to her paid room, not even wanting to stay the night. Marlene was amazed, and she thought God had answered her prayers. At the time, she had never heard of telepathy.

Simple thought transference—telepathy without the possibility of other explanation—works best when there is a compelling reason for it. If there is an emotional urgency in transmitting a message, or if normal means of communication are out, then it works even better.

Experimental Telepathy

Stress is by no means the only thing that can bring about communication from mind to mind. To a degree, telepathy can be induced experimentally as well. One classic series of telepathy experiments involved a noted Australian explorer, Sir Hubert Wilkins, and a Little Rock, Arkansas, psychic named Harold Sherman.

> During Sir Hubert's travels to the Arctic, he was to transmit information about himself to Sherman daily, and Sherman was to take down whatever he received. The material would then be compared after Sir Hubert came back to New York. To ensure the integrity of the results, a team of researchers stood by whenever Sherman was getting messages telepathically.
> On one such occasion, which took place in a New York hotel room, Sherman insisted that he saw (telepathically, that is) Sir Hubert dancing in formal evening clothes. This seemed particularly improbable; at the time, the explorer was due at the Arctic base of his expedition. But when Sir Hubert returned to New York, it was learned that en route to the Arctic base, his plane had been forced down in a snowstorm and had landed in Calgary, the capital of the Canadian province of Alberta. It so happened that the governor of Alberta was being inaugurated that day, and shortly after Sir Hubert's unscheduled arrival, the inaugural ball took place. The governor invited Sir Hubert to come and lent him a suit to wear. Thus, what Sherman had seen thousands of miles away in New York was indeed correct.

Some years later, telepathic experimentation was taken to even greater heights.

Apollo 14 astronaut Edgar D. Mitchell attempted to send mental messages from space to a Chicago engineer whose hobby was extrasensory perception. Using ESP cards, Mitchell proved that telepathy can work even from the outer reaches of space. The experiment became part of the history of parapsychology, and Mitchell became an active experimenter in ESP.

In scientific language, "cross-correspondences" are controlled experiments, often long-distance, in which a psychic person gets impressions of situations while teams of scientific observers at both ends also record what they see or what is happening. There are many well-documented cases of this.

Other Forms of Telepathy

Another form of telepathy, somewhat different from both spontaneous urgency telepathy and experimentally induced telepathy, involves communication between the unconscious mind of a sleeping person and the conscious mind of a person who is fully awake.

J.S., a college student from Cleveland, went to the library to do some research. Suddenly, she heard a friend, Brian, call her name. She looked around for him but could not find him. Then she heard him call her name again, as though he were standing next to her, and he asked if he could come in. She looked again, and realized that Brian was not in the library. She then looked at the time. It was two o'clock in the afternoon.

When she got home, she found Brian asleep on the couch in her living room. He awoke and asked where she had been. She told him, and asked him in return where *he* had been at two o'clock. He replied he had gotten off work at about one, and shortly after that had come over to see if there was anyone home at her house. He had called her name outside the house, but when no one answered he opened the door, called again, and asked if he could come in. No one was home, so he lay down on the couch and took a nap.

Some individuals are sufficiently skilled in utilizing their telepathic talents that they can act as "operators" for messages to and from other people.

> Several years ago, I was at a play rehearsal in New York when I suddenly remembered that I had made an appointment with a friend for five o'clock that evening. The set was closed and there was no telephone nearby, and I became increasingly unhappy at the thought of having to disappoint him. One of the singers present—a psychically gifted young lady—noticed my preoccupation. I explained the situation, and expressed my wish to send my friend a message to that effect.
>
> "Is that all?" the singer asked. She closed her eyes for a moment, breathed deeply, and then, reopening her eyes, said, "The message has been delivered."
>
> I laughed a little uncertainly, and went on with the work at hand. When I returned home around six o'clock, I telephoned my friend and started to apologize for not having called him earlier.
>
> "What are you talking about?" he said. "My answering service told me someone called at five o'clock to say you'd be delayed."

Finally, in considering types of telepathy, I would like to point out that stage performers who call themselves "mentalists" and claim to be able to read people's minds are almost never doing this, and they are certainly *not* engaged in telepathy. The majority of mentalists are clever entertainers, nothing more, even if they practice their skills on ordinary audience members rather than hired "plants" posing as such (a not-uncommon practice). Occasionally, some genuine ESP is involved, but in fact these entertainers are most often the first to deny this. There is no evidence that anyone can "read" another person's mind (although there is evidence that a person's thoughts can be caught by another person, especially if he or she is close by). "Mind-reading" is not telepathy.

THE USES OF TELEPATHY

What can telepathy do for you? Lots of things. If you are "aware"—that is, willing to accept messages of this kind—you may well be warned in times of danger by someone at a distance who wishes you well. Conversely, you may do this favor for someone yourself. It is a distinct thrill when people who are very close, such as husband and wife or two good friends, manage to communicate without words—spoken words, that is. Not because it saves wear and tear on their vocal cords, but because the spark of instant thought flying from mind to mind can make a relationship stronger. When creative work is involved, the separate thought processes of two writers or two artists can be fused into one creative effort!

In business, it can be very useful for the executive or sales representative to catch a fleeting thought from the mind of the person across the table. As noted before, this is not mind-reading, but merely being tuned in to what the other person wishes to put across. Just imagine how surprised your new boss would be if you spontaneously came out with the very thing he had on his mind! On the other hand, if the person you are dealing with is likely to be unreliable, catching a thought wave might very well warn you to be careful.

I do not pretend that everybody can use telepathy in the same way. But *potentially*, at least, it is a lost faculty that can be restored to us if we assume the proper attitude, and then allow our telepathic ability to improve by actually using it.

TAPPING YOUR TELEPATHIC POTENTIAL

Practically speaking, telepathy is a faculty we all may have deeply embedded within our personalities, but, in general, only those of us who are naturally "good senders" or "good receivers" make practical use of this most valuable talent. However, there are ways you can explore—and develop—your own abilities in this area. There are basically two ways of doing this, one a bit more formal than the other.

If you choose the first, more formal, approach, first enlist a suitable partner. This should be someone you know at least fairly well (it is extremely difficult to send out a thought message to someone you cannot visualize) and who, like you, is honestly interested and not afraid of what might happen. It makes no difference whether the two of you are in different rooms in the same apartment or a thousand miles apart; telepathy does not recognize the difference.

Plan on holding regular sessions of perhaps half an hour each, during which a predetermined number (ten is a good place to begin) of ideas or images are sent. Keep a record on each end as to what is sent and what is received. Each person may function alternately as sender and receiver, or each may adopt one of these roles exclusively. Do not discuss the substance of your messages before the session is held. After the session is over, compare the two records.

The second approach to experimenting with telepathy is more informal and more closely imitates the way this faculty normally works in everyday life. Visualize the person to whom you wish to transmit your thoughts. Then contact the other person at intervals to see if he or she has received your message, but do so without mentioning the fact that you are attempting to send one. If the other person is aware of your efforts, he or she may tense up, making it twice as hard to get through. If the receiver does not know when and what will be transmitted telepathically, you are more likely to have an open door on the other end.

Whichever approach you choose, try to let go of preconceived notions as to whether your experiment will "work" or not. Cautious optimism—that it may well work—is the best attitude to take. Above all, relax, and don't strain or force. Tension is your enemy. A carefree, unperturbed, and, above all, unhurried attitude is helpful. It is important that you cultivate a calm state of mind, and be in reasonably good physical health and comfortable. Noise and other distractions tend to interfere with transmission. Start by transmitting, or trying to transmit, relatively simple messages or thoughts. These may be sentences or they may be simple visual images.

Generally speaking, if the receiver fully (or nearly so) identifies three or more out of ten possible messages, you have beaten the law of averages and scored in ESP. Incidentally, it is unlikely that you will score ten out of ten. Also, some messages may be obscured in part, or they may be received out of sequence. Thought transference happens outside the conventional time stream; therefore, the sequence of messages can be jumbled, since all of them exist together in the timeless dimension.

Finally, do not impose rigid time demands on your experiments—for instance, don't insist that it must work by next week or else. Let yourself go, allow it to happen, and sooner or later, it may. The more you relax-and-project (instead of concentrate-and-worry), the more chance you will have of coming across from mind to mind—and the more you practice, chances are, the more successful you will be.

3

FORETELLING THE FUTURE

Nothing fascinates people more than the ability some have to foretell future events. The desire to know what lies ahead is a natural human instinct, not just idle curiosity. Many serious people, even leading business executives and professionals of one kind or another, consult psychics regularly in the hope of getting advance information, or warnings, so that they can act accordingly.

The ability to have accurate information about events, situations, and people before we become consciously aware of them is known as precognition. Next to telepathic communication between living persons, incidents of precognition are the most common psychic experiences. In the days of the Bible these were referred to as prophecies; in their least desirable form, they are called fortunetelling (though, heaven knows, the fortune made is usually that of the fortuneteller). Again, the basic characteristic of the phenomenon is that information is obtained in seeming disregard of the conventional boundaries of time and space. Distance in either time or geography has no effect on the results of this faculty. Precognition flies directly in the face of established reality as most people define it.

I am convinced that precognition is one faculty with three different forms of expression. The form it takes depends on the particular phase of the psychic person—that is, the area in which an individual's psychic talent manifests itself. Just as some musicians are good on the piano while others are better with a violin and still others are singers, so we have people who foresee things, others who hear things before they happen, and still others (though relatively few in number) who can get olfactory impressions—smells with particular associations. I consider all three of these faculties a step more advanced than telepathy because they involve insight into the future—or, at the very least, beyond great distance.

CLAIRVOYANCE

The ability to see future events is known as *clairvoyance*; a person who possesses this talent is a *clairvoyant*. The word, of French origin, means "seeing clearly"—that is to say, seeing clearly that which most people cannot see at all. Among those who practice precognition, clairvoyants are by far the most numerous. Clairvoyance is sometimes also called "second sight."

Clairvoyants' visions can be subjective (in the mind's eye) or objective (seeming to appear before them). Every *honest* fortuneteller, every capable medium, and every person able to have strong and accurate hunches about future events comes under this heading. (Note that sometimes a psychic person is called a sensitive, sometimes a medium or mediumistic, and sometimes merely a psychic; these terms mean exactly the same thing and can be used interchangeably.) Clairvoyance, even more than telepathy, cannot be produced at will, and the flashes of sudden insight or meaningful dreams should always be considered important events.

CLAIRAUDIENCE

Clairaudience is the ability to hear voices or messages that foretell the future. Usually, a person with this ability speaks of hearing the messages in his or her inner ear, without seeing the person who speaks.

A clairaudient person will hear a voice "in his head" (or near it), as clearly as if the sender were right next to the receiver. If an individual hears the voice of a dead person, this suggests that such a person is in fact doing the talking, especially if the hearer recognizes the voice. No amount of tortured "explanation" by people to whom the reality of the Other Side of Life is unacceptable will alter this simple fact.

> About twelve years ago, my brother's father-in-law died suddenly of a heart attack. He was a man who had no belief in psychic phenomena or life beyond this dimension. His death left his widow distraught and unprepared to cope, although she tried to adjust. Several weeks after the funeral, I was making coffee in my kitchen when I suddenly heard a male voice, seemingly next to my head, urgently calling out my name. I checked the rest of our large apartment—there was no one there. I dismissed the matter. The following day, at precisely the same time, the voice came again, even more urgently, and this time I knew whose voice it was. It was my brother's late father-in-law. I picked up the telephone and called his widow. As it turned out, she was making serious plans to commit suicide at that moment. Fortunately, when I told her what had happened, her outlook changed considerably.

CLAIRSENTIENCE

The third form of cognitive activity transcending the conventional barriers of time and space is *clairsentience*, the ability to smell scents that others, who are not psychic, cannot register. This form of psychic talent is probably the rarest of the three phases of precognition, and the least capable of scientific verification, but it nevertheless exists and we must reckon with it.

I have a fair amount of this faculty myself. Whether it is due to my prominent Austrian nose or merely to my generally acute sensitivity in other areas, I don't know, but I have on occasion registered smells that others were unable to detect.

> Many years ago, I accepted an invitation to visit with an amateur medium at her home in Brooklyn, New York, to explore her abilities. She had met me at a lecture on psychic subjects

and had talked to me without realizing that I was a psychical researcher and author. There was no money involved, and she knew very little about me or my family.

Bertha was a widow living on a pension. There was nothing remarkable about her somewhat plump person. Her apartment was comfortable and convenient, but devoid of anything special in the way of style or beauty. In the living room with the two of us were two other people who were friends of hers. We turned out most of the lights and Bertha became clairvoyant. As she was "reading"—that is, mentioning names, places, and situations that she felt coming into her consciousness—I was relaxing in a deep easy chair, not thinking of anything or anyone in particular. I am not at all keen on the idea of "contacting" loved ones at will, and, besides, I was present strictly as an observer.

Suddenly, I sensed a strong smell of lily of the valley right in front of my face. I started to look around as best I could in the darkened room to see if there were any flowers about, when Bertha announced that my mother had "come in" and wanted me to know she was present. This I found extremely interesting, as my mother's favorite perfume, and also her favorite flower, had been the lily of the valley. As soon as we turned on the lights, I carefully examined the room and Bertha's clothes, and I stepped close to each of her two friends. No one had on any perfume or any scent remotely similar to lily of the valley. Furthermore, only I had registered the scent!

The value of being clairvoyant or clairaudient is clear—they are ways of learning about impending dangers or conditions, and while forewarned may not always be forearmed, it can be helpful to know what lies ahead, regardless of the final outcome. But it is not so clear with clairsentience, which is rarely capable of delivering a clearly understandable "message." While clairsentience can be useful at times, most of the scientifically reliable data on precognition come from reports of the other types of precognition. I think that the chief value of clairsentience, in the main, is in helping to more clearly identify the source of a psychic message. You may not fully recognize a personality by a first name, but if a particular scent is re-created—a scent that is or was closely associated with a certain person—you will probably find it more possible to identify the individual and accept that he or she is the source of a psychic communication.

THE NATURE OF PRECOGNITION

The majority of precognitive experiences—whether clairvoyance, clairaudience, or clairsentience—occur spontaneously and are unsought. Some people have an inkling of a precognitive situation shortly before it occurs—they may feel odd, experience a sensation of giddiness or tingling in various parts of the body, or simply have a vague foreboding. For others, precognitive experiences come entirely out of left field, surprising and unexpected.

I have spoken with a number people who think that they are "evil witches" because they "saw" an accident or the death of a friend or loved one, and it later happened exactly as they foresaw it. But a receiver no more controls what he or she foretells than a television set controls the programming that comes through it. There are cases on record in which thought concentrations may have caused people to be influenced at a distance, sometimes even making them do things not consciously in their will, but this requires a conscious and deliberate effort—usually by several people working together. This type of undertaking lacks the spontaneity generally associated with true precognitive experiences, which come upon one suddenly and last for only a short time.

There is some question as to whether persons with psychic ability foresee the future around certain individuals or independent of specific persons. I believe that if a number of predictions are made about a single individual by a number of seers independently of one another, then the future event must cling to the aura, or electromagnetic energy, of the individual about whom the predictions are made. If, on the other hand, a number of seers foretell a future event without reference to a particular individual or individuals, then it would appear that a channel has been opened into an event in the future in which those concerned merely play a part—a part over which they have no control.

Intuition and Hunches

The ability to look into the future is an ability that is present in every one of us, whether we know it or not. However, there are different degrees of this ability. In its most primitive form, it is the instinct or intuition that makes us sense danger or love or warmth, and react accordingly.

A higher form of the same ability is the hunch. At this stage, actual psychic ability begins. A hunch is a basically "illogical" feeling about a person or situation that nevertheless influences your thinking and actions. To follow a hunch is to go against purely logical reasoning.

A hunch that turns out to be correct is a type of extrasensory knowledge. A hunch that turns out to be false may not have been a hunch at all, but rather a feeling of fear. The two can feel very much alike. Fear of failure, for instance, can frequently masquerade as a hunch of impending disaster. But a true hunch carries with it a sense of immediacy—it appears suddenly and lasts only a short time—whereas fear is a more lingering or extended feeling.

Premonitions

A premonition is a form of precognitive experience that is more definite than a hunch but less specific (and much more common) than the more complex types of foreknowledge. Premonitions are usually feelings about events to come rather than sharply defined flashes of actual scenes or events.

> Michael Bentine, a British television personality, actor, and comedian with strong psychic inclinations, once scheduled a sketch dealing with a Welsh coal-mining village to run on an October installment of his regular television program. For reasons unknown to him, however, he felt it just wasn't right and decided to cancel the sketch at the last minute. On the day the sketch would have run, a huge heap of mining refuse buried the Welsh village of Aberfan, killing 138 people, many of them children.

Eugene Thompson, an attorney in St. Paul, Minnesota, was accused of the murder of his wife. The accusation rested largely on the fact that he had recently taken out a large amount of life insurance on his wife's life. His explanation for this was that he had foreseen the event. Almost a year before his wife was murdered, he had told a friend he had a terrible premonition that "Carol would meet with some tragic accident" within a year. Thompson, who had a history of clairvoyant experiences—one, in childhood, involving the death of a sister in an automobile accident—then took out two insurance policies on his wife's life, and he told his insurance agent about his premonition. He saw his wife's death as occurring on February 8th or 9th of the following year, and when the date passed, he should have been relieved. But less than a month later, she was stabbed to death.

I read the testimony in this latter case, and I greatly doubt that Thompson could have committed the crime he was accused of. If he had been involved in the manner the state claimed he was, he would surely have had some misgivings about his own role in the tragedy. It is extremely unlikely that he would not have foreseen his own commission of a crime while foreseeing the death of his own wife.

Sometimes people have premonitions of impending events without realizing it. They may say strange things to friends or relatives, that later, in retrospect, assume different meanings.

In July of 1965, Adlai Stevenson, then U.S. Ambassador to the United Nations, left for a trip to London. Asked when he expected to return, Stevenson replied, without a moment's hesitation, "If I survive this trip, I'll be back in three weeks." He didn't—he died of a heart attack while overseas.

Probably the most publicized premonition in recent history concerned the assassination of President John F. Kennedy, which took place on November 22, 1963.

Jeane Dixon, a Washington real-estate dealer and a highly talented psychic, had long been startling friends and acquaintances with uncanny predictions that had, often unfortunately, come true. As early as 1956, she had predicted that the 1960 presidential election would be won by a Democrat who would die in office. By November of 1963, Dixon was experiencing increasing feelings of foreboding concerning the president—the Massachusetts Democrat who had won the 1960 election. The Sunday before the assassination, she said, she felt a "black veil" closing in on the White House, and it continued to draw closer in the following days. On Tuesday, she told her luncheon companions, "Dear God, something terrible is going to happen to the president, soon." On Friday, President Kennedy was murdered in Dallas.

Most premonitions concern disasters or negative aspects of life, and people often dismiss these impressions or actively suppress them because they are afraid or reluctant to be the bearers of bad news. As a result, much valuable psychic material is undoubtedly lost to science, and where there might have been warnings—and possibly prevention of disaster or harm—there is only the *fait accompli.*

Complex Precognitive Experiences

Beyond intuition, hunches, and premonitions lies the ability to actually foresee or foretell future events or situations, or, in some cases, to see events or situations that are happening a distance away. Here too there are a variety of stages or degrees.

There is, first of all, the experience of foreseeing or foretelling an encounter with either a situation or a person without "getting" any specifics as to time and place. For instance, one day you may suddenly find yourself thinking about someone you haven't seen or thought about for years and then, soon afterward, you run into that person. If such a simple precognitive experience occurs in the dream or sleep state, it may be surrounded by, or couched in, symbolic language, with parallel situations representing the message itself. For example, you may have a precognitive dream in which your brother has bought a new car that he wants to show you. The following day, your brother calls to ask if he can visit you in the near future, and when he arrives, it turns out that he has just remarried and wants you to meet his bride. The new car in the dream was a symbol for your brother's new wife. Simple precognitive messages received in the waking condition generally contain much more precise descriptive material, although they still may not contain the details of time, place, and description that you might wish for.

Next in the range of precognitive experiences comes the impression in which information as to time or place is included. This may be only partial, such as numeral "flashed" above the face of someone who appears in a precognitive vision, or a key word spoken by an inner voice that relates to the circumstances under which an event will take place. Depending upon the individual personality of the receiver and his or her state of relaxation at the time of the experience, the precognitive message will be more or less involved.

> In early autumn, 1967, Lorna Middleton, a London piano teacher, felt a strong premonition that Robert F. Kennedy—brother of the late president and a Democratic Senator from New York—would be killed. On March 15, 1968, she actually saw the assassination take place, and felt it happening while the senator was on tour in the West. This impression was followed by another one on April 5, and again on April 11. On the night of June 5, Kennedy, then seeking the Democratic Party's nomination for the presidency, was murdered.

> Allen Hencher, a forty-five-year-old telephone worker with distinct psychic ability, was awake all night with an ominous headache of the type he had come to associate with his precognitive experiences. As he lay in his bed, he clearly foresaw an airplane crash in which there would be 124 victims. He said the scene reminded him of Greece, and described in detail some statuary around a church that appeared in his vision. Several weeks later, there was an airplane crash on the island of Cyprus in the eastern Mediterranean. One hundred and twenty-four people were killed.

Precognitive messages concerning matters that are merely routine (although possibly of some emotional significance to the receiver) are less likely to contain dramatic descriptive detail than messages dealing with catastrophes, warnings of dire events, or matters of importance to more than one individual. Those who are able to foretell plane crashes, for instance (a specialty among some clairvoyants), often do so with a great deal of detail. Fires and earthquakes also seem to evoke graphic images in the consciousness of those able to foretell them.

The curious thing, of course, is that not all such occurrences take place exactly as predicted. In fact, about half of all predictions made by basically honest psychics and readers are not entirely accurate with regard to dates. (I know this because I have kept statistical charts of predictions made over a period of several years by about a dozen genuine psychics.) This is because visionaries often completely lack correct judgment of the time element—not surprising, since the messages in question come from a timeless dimension (more about this in Chapter 4). This does not make them less valid as precognitive experiences; it only demonstrates some of the properties of the reality beyond the physical.

THE USES OF PRECOGNITION

Unless we are aficionados of ESP, most of us tend to disregard, or at least play down, any psychic predictions or warnings that come our way. Eastern philosophers may argue the question of *karma*—that is, the idea that credits or demerits from a previous lifetime follow you into your present life—and say that it is your karma that determines whether or not you will heed a given warning. Perhaps this is true, but it seems to me largely a matter of personality.

How much stock should the average person put in predictions? To the minority of people who have taken precognition warnings seriously, it has often proved a boon.

When Mildred Liebowitz was a teenager growing up in Brooklyn, New York, she wanted a radio in her bedroom. Not having space to put in on a dresser or night table, she had a shelf hung above her bed and placed the radio there. One night several months later, Mildred's mother could not sleep. She kept seeing her daughter's arm against the wall, with the electric cord from the radio wrapped around it. Then she saw her daugher turn, pulling the radio down on her head. Finally, she got up and went into Mildred's room and, sure enough, Mildred's arm was against the wall with the electric cord wrapped around it. One more move on her part would have brought the radio crashing down on her head.

Royce Wight, a young Florida man, was taking a nap in his bedroom when he suddenly woke up and dashed out of the room. Seconds later, a three-ton concrete piling from a construction site adjacent to his home crashed through the roof. "I had a premonition of trouble," he was quoted as saying.

A well-known television personality had a premonition that something terrible was going to happen when she set out on her weekly trip to New York. As she got into her car in the Hamptons, she reportedly said, "This trip is doomed. I wish I didn't have to make it." As she was driving to the city, her car skidded out of control, hit another car, and killed a woman.

The woman in the last story did not know who would be the victim, only that something terrible would happen. Since a clairvoyant person usually sees events as a whole, rather than individual actions that come together to create these events, it can be impossible to heed such a warning unless you call off a contemplated event altogether.

I have been asked whether true clairvoyants should not be able to use their talents to foresee all the difficulties, dangers, and opportunities they may encounter, and so avoid everything negative and take advantage of the positive. Whether fortunately or unfortunately, it has been my experience that psychics are almost never able to read for themselves. I cannot say why, but it may be because they are too close to their subjects, and unconsciously fear that their own personality and conscious knowledge might interfere with their psychic reading. Or there may be some psychic law operating here that we understand only in part.

TAPPING YOUR PRECOGNITIVE POTENTIAL

Is there anything we can do to enhance our ability to foretell the future? Definitely, yes. First of all, it is more likely for a person who has had some indication of this talent to be able to increase it than for a person who has never had a precognitive experience to be able to develop it. But the technique to use is pretty much the same in either case. Basically, it consists of a state of watchfulness toward any indication, no matter how slight, that a premonition is about to take place. Nothing must be ignored; everything should be written down and, if possible, reputable witnesses should be alerted as to the nature of the premonition as soon as it is received. Another method of recording predictions is to write yourself a letter concerning the experience and mail it to yourself by registered mail, thus permitting the postmark to act as a guarantee concerning the time of the prediction.

As for increasing your ability to have premonitory experiences, you should always maintain an attitude of acceptance, regardless of whether the material you obtain is pleasant or unpleasant. An absence of fear and a certain objectivity concerning the material are equally necessary. Morally, you are required to pass on whatever information you receive, whether it is good or bad.

If you want to obtain specific information concerning the future, there are certain inducing agents that may work. If the object of your interest is someone other than yourself, a photograph of the person or even his or her name written in clear letters on a piece of paper may serve as a concentration point. Once you have visualized the person or object of your search into the future, settle back in as relaxed a state as possible and concentrate upon the person or object. This process resembles meditation, except that a precise channeling of thought should take place. If tangential thoughts occur, dismiss them; if your mind wanders off, bring it back at once to the topic at hand.

Be aware, however, that these exercises are aimed at helping you to become tuned in to any precognitive messages you receive. They cannot make you receive them. As we have seen, the precognitive experience is usually unexpected, and certainly cannot be forced. Of course, just being tuned in to your feelings and hunches can make a tremendous difference, since so often our first impulse is to ignore or repress any such messages. It is possible that you may have received, and may still be receiving, messages concerning the future, but (consciously or unconsciously) have chosen to ignore them. If you utilize the above suggestions, you may find you have more psychic ability than you ever thought possible.

4

THE REALITY OF TIME AND PSYCHIC ABILITY

Knowledge of what lies ahead allows you to prepare for future events in one way or another. But what makes the ability to foretell future events more controversial and tantalizing than any other aspect of ESP goes somewhat deeper. Specifically, an event that has not yet come into being is something that the ordinary person cannot perceive, or even conceive—something that we would say does not exist and therefore has no reality. Yet hundreds of thousands of people have been able to describe in great detail situations and happenings that come to pass only at a future date. Thus, the existence of precognition makes it obvious that our concepts of time and the sequence of events is in need of some revision. Either our sense of time is wrong or events themselves are predestined by some superior law with which we are not yet fully familiar.

It is very difficult to judge such matters from within this dimension, and it is quite impossible for anyone to be totally outside of it at any time. We must therefore construct a theory that will allow for the existence of so many experiences pertaining to the so-called future while at the same time still being consistent with what we know about life on earth and the time-space continuum.

TIME AND EVENTS

First, let it be stated that time, as we know it, is a human convenience that gives us a point of reference and a structure within which to understand our experiences. Events, meanwhile, appear to be predestined, to a large degree, by a system that I call the Universal Law. Now, this Universal Law is not something you can look up in law books or consult your lawyer (or even your minister) about. Rather, the term implies an orderly dimension beyond our physical world that is governed by rules and regulations. The concept of Universal Law is based not on abstract belief but on the study and correlation of material obtained in literally thousands of psychic readings, interviews, trance sesions, and other forms of communication between the "world next door" (as celebrated medium Eileen Garrett used to call it) and this, our world.

One aspect of the Universal Law governs communications between our world and the timeless dimension. For instance, genuine spirit communication is always limited, that is, there is always a point when the contact must come to an end. The Universal Law, however, goes beyond the mechanics of communication. I have found that it addresses the moral actions or attitudes of people through various types of rewards and retribution. It is also at work in the relationship between time and events, which is actually quite different than many of us imagine.

Many people who have the ability to foretell future events find it more of a burden than a blessing. They may also begin to believe that because they foretell bad events, they may in some way be involved in causing them. This, of course, is not true. By picking up signals as to that which lies ahead, receivers merely act as channels for communicating what the future holds.

The Nature of Time

The conventional view concerning the sequence of events and the time-space continuum holds that the past is followed by the present, which in turn is followed by the future. The sequence cannot be reversed, this theory holds, nor can anyone get from the past into the future without going through the present.

Against this view stand thousands upon thousands of verified cases in which people have foreseen future events in great detail long before these events became objective reality. Whether the foreknowledge is of events that occur one minute later or a year afterward is of no importance, because, as we shall see, we are dealing with a dimension in which time, as we define it, does not exist.

The foretelling of future events is not an isolated instance involving some extraordinarily gifted individual; it is a fairly common occurrence among many types of people—men and women, young and old, rich and poor, people living in every country on earth. It has occurred in the past, and it continues to occur daily. It is, in fact, an expression of a natural part of the human personality. It is not the same with everyone, to be sure, but the ability to break through the time and space barrier is inherent in human nature. So we must somehow find a scientific structure that fits conditions as they exist, rather than continuing to try to force paranormal occurrences to conform to our existing "laws" of science. Otherwise, science becomes a lie.

Cause and Effect

Assuming, then, that foreseeing the future is a natural phenomenon, we must conclude that the conventional view concerning the nature of time is incorrect. There must be an explanation as to why people with psychic ability can leave the time stream temporarily—stick their heads outside of it, as it were—to look into the so-called future or past and come up with information they could not have learned through the ordinary five senses. The only logical explanation for this is the existence of a timeless dimension in which events are preordained in general terms, put in place by a variety of circumstances.

This calls for a very involved and sophisticated law of cause and effect, far beyond that which we, in the three-dimensional physical world, normally call by that name. In this timeless dimension, the great patterns of events are set in motion long before we reach their place in the time stream.

The events themselves are stationary, and we are in motion toward them. We meet up with specific events by what some call fate, some call God's will, and others, like me, prefer to call the Universal Law. When we so encounter an event, we say that the event has happened to us. At that point, we have a number of alternatives: We can ignore it; we can run from it; or we can move toward it positively, actively. Depending upon our initiative, one of several consequences will result, leading, in turn, to a new set of events in the distance.

In some cases, foreknowledge of a developing situation serves only as a warning, and events can be altered by conscious effort. Other events cannot be altered, although advance notice of them can help us to prepare for them. Whichever is the case, there is within us an extrasensory faculty that enables us, under certain conditions, to pierce the barriers of time and space—to look around corners, as it were.

> Barbara M., a California woman, decided to drive up the coast with some friends. They were about twenty-five or thirty miles from town when Barbara felt that something terrible would happen if they went much farther. She insisted that they go back. Her friends asked why, and she told them that if they went much farther, they would be involved in an automobile accident. The next day, Barbara read in the newspaper of an accident that had happened approximately five minutes after they had turned around, not more than a few miles farther up the road. Two cars were totally wrecked, and all the people in them, about six, were killed instantly. The next day, Barbara and her friends decided to check out a rather morbid idea. They drove back up the coast at the same speed, and determined that if they had gone on, they would have been in exactly the wrong place at the wrong time, and very likely would have been involved in the accident, too.

In this example, which is typical of this type of phenomenon, a number of individuals, including Barbara, were in a certain place on the time track and were racing toward a rendezvous with death. But because Barbara was in tune with her psychic ability, she sensed the event before coming to it. Recognizing her hunch and then choosing to act upon it (which are two different things), she made a positive decision, and was saved. In an instance of this kind, psychic ability is used not to actually foresee a future event, but to see the *tendency toward* a certain event at a point at which an individual can still do something about it, at least as far as his or her own participation in it is concerned. Thus, Barbara did not prevent the accident, but was able to alter her own behavior so as to avoid becoming involved in it.

FUTURE AND PAST

If future time as we know it can be penetrated by some with psychic ability before it becomes objective reality for us, would not the same apply to time that has receded into the past? Can we actually step into the past, as it were, and obtain information, even have experiences, we would not normally be familiar with? It seems that some people can.

Just as the future, which is "not yet," can be viewed from the present, so too can the past, which is "no more." Though artifacts from distant periods in the past may still remain, the past itself is gone. The events shaping it and the people who inhabited it are no longer in existence in the physical sense of the word. There is, however, one basic difference between the past and the future. The future is not yet, when seen from the present, and therefore has no realistic existence in terms of the ordinary five senses. The past, on the other hand, has had a realistic existence, and therefore has a "track record" of having been at one time.

THE SUBJECTIVENESS OF TIME

All of these concepts relating to time can be difficult for us to talk about, or even to grasp. However, the difficulty in coming to terms with them lies not so much in the limitations of our ordinary five senses as in the terminology we force ourselves to use. Because we divide our consciousness into three distinct segments—past, present, and future—we arbitrarily cut a steady flow of consciousness into separate and distinct units. In actuality, the progression from past to present to future is continuous and uninterrupted. It is also relative to the observer—that is to say, a particular spot in the time stream goes from being the future to being the present to being the past, depending upon where you stand in relation to it. In essence, past, present, and future are made of the same stuff. The dividers between them are artificial and flexible.

Thus, when I speak of the past, this should be taken as subjective in the sense that it is the past *as seen from my individual point of view.* Individual points of view may be similar among large groups of people—even the entire human population—but they are nevertheless nothing more than the sum total of individual observations.

Thus, it might be more correct to speak of past events as *accomplished events.* By contrast, future events might be characterized as *unrealized events.* The reality of past and future events is identical; only their relationships to the observer differ. From the point of view of the observer, past events have occurred and can no longer be altered. Future events exist independently but have not yet occurred in relationship to the observer, and may conceivably be altered, at least in some instances.

EXPLORING OTHER TIMES

There are several ways in which we can actually transport ourselves, or parts of ourselves at least, into the so-called past. One of them is psychometry, in which you derive impressions from an object, person, or place that give you information about events that took place some time before. In psychometry, you read a kind of emotional photograph of past events. In reconstructing an event through psychometric impulses, and with the help of the conscious mind, you do not actually recreate the event itself, but merely read an imprint or copy of it. This is, however, sufficient to derive information about an event and thus learn facts that might otherwise be lost in history. (A more detailed discussion of psychometry will be found in Chapter 5.)

In a book entitled *Window to the Past* (Citadel Press, 1993), I showed how a psychicially gifted person can be taken to historical "hot spots"—places where puzzles in history have not been fully resolved—and attempt psychometry to resolve pending issues. The great medium Sybil Leek was thus able to pinpoint the location of Camelot in England and the site of the first Viking landings on Cape Cod in Massachusetts. In this application, psychic ability can be a very valuable tool for historical exploration, especially when all other means of historical research have failed. Information obtained this way is not used as a direct source of historical information, but as a point of departure for conventional historical research.

A second method of visiting the past is astral projection, also called "out-of-body experience," in which the etheric body (the inner self) temporarily leaves the physical body and travels, usually at great speed, to other places. Ordinarily, astral projection involves travel in space rather than in time. It is, however, also possible to direct astral projection into a predetermined place in past history. This works best if it is done at the physical location you wish to investigate, but it can also be done from a distance away. The success of such an experiment depends upon your power of visualization and the absence of interference from conscious or unconscious sources. (A more detailed discussion of astral projection will be found in Chapter 6.)

Somewhere on the borderline between astral projection and psychometry lies a phenomenon called "traveling clairvoyance." In traveling clairvoyance, part of the psychic is projected outward and is able to observe conditions as they existed in the past without actually leaving his or her physical body. This, however, is a talent found primarily in professional mediums and those with a great deal of experience in controlling the ways in which their psychic talents manifest themselves. It is not an easily acquired talent.

Hypnotic regression, as it is used in connection with reincarnation research, can also propel an individual into the past. This can be a means of getting information from past incarnations that can be verified independently afterward. Since hypnotic regression is more concerned with personal experiences in past lives than with historical exploration, the thrust of the investigation is somewhat different from that required for purely past-oriented research. (More about hypnotic regression in Chapter 7.)

THE "TIME WARP" PHENOMENON

There are a number of instances on record in which people have accidentally entered a "time warp"—that is to say, an area (in either the mental or physical sense—or both) in which a different time stream was still extant.

> A young man driving from northern Oregon to California came around a bend in the road and suddenly found himself in the middle of a blizzard, although he had left in August, when the weather was extremely hot. For what seemed to him a full day, he found himself in a mining town among people dressed in clothes of the early 1900s. He spoke to them and found them to be three-dimensional people. Suddenly, he was seized by panic. Regaining the safety of his automobile, he drove away, to the bewilderment of those he left behind. Shortly afterward, he found himself back again in the present and the relative comfort of a hot August day.

Many people's first reaction to this story would be that the young man was obviously hallucinating or dreaming. Yet one cannot necessarily classify all such experiences as hallucinations. In the case of this young man, his detailed descriptions of his encounter seem to indicate that he did indeed enter a time warp of sorts. Whether this was due to his own psychic abilities or to the location at which he encountered the phenomenon is difficult to assess. From time to time, similar cases have been reported in which people, and even vehicles, from the past have been observed amid contemporary scenes, only to vanish a few moments later and, sometimes, to return on other occasions or to other observers.

Physicists have long pointed out that energy cannot dissipate, but must continue to exist, even if it is transmuted or otherwise changed in form. Could it not be that emotionally tinged scenes—which, after all, represent energy—exist in a dimension not ordinarily accessible to us for observation? Then, on occasion, certain individuals are able to penetrate into this dimension, where past events continue to move on a different time track from the one we currently acknowledge as the "present," and the scenes reappear, if only briefly.

Thus, walking into the past can be a matter of choice or a matter of accident. Either way, the past is far from dead, and continues to intermingle with our present. The kind of psychic ability that permits a person to tell facts about a person or place without having access to any information or conscious knowledge of the person or place is very common, so it must be assumed that the past continues to exist all around us—that is to say, it exudes tiny particles of itself that those who are sufficiently sensitive may pick up and derive information from.

FOREKNOWLEDGE, FREE WILL, AND FATE

One thing is certain: If thousands upon thousands of people have correctly foreseen events before they occured, then these events must have been "planned ahead" of the moment at which they happen. To me there is no other logical explanation but that there is a Universal Law operating in this world—and also in the neighboring one, which is invisible to all but the psychic. To me, fate is not an all-powerful force, but an intelligent, just system in which the individual is neither pawn nor power, but partner; what you make of your opportunities determines your progress.

This may sound cruel and unjust, especially when apparently innocent people suffer or are killed in tragedies. And, indeed, only the concept of reincarnation, with its karmic laws of reward and punishment, offers a *logical* explanation for these apparent inequities. But as Carl Jung, who pioneered the psychology of the unconscious, pointed out, there is another law, beyond the law of cause and effect, called the law of *meaningful coincidence,* that comes into play in our universe.

> Max and Pauline Elsasser, a New Jersey couple in their late fifties, decided to drive down to Florida for their annual vacation instead of flying, as they had done for years. Before they left, Mrs. Elsasser told her son that she didn't want to go because she was sure "something" was going to happen. But the Florida vacation had become part of their way of life, so they left their home in Weehawken, picked up another couple on the way, and headed for Florida. As they were driving on U.S. Route 301, eight miles west of Marion, South Carolina, their car went out of control and slammed into a bridge wall on the divided highway. The four occupants were killed instantly. There was no other traffic on the road, and the weather was clear and dry. The only possible explanation for the crash was that the setting sun might have blinded Mr. Elsasser, who was driving.

In such a situation, what are we to think about the other couple? Had they been brought together with the Elsassers because their fates were to be united? Was someone pulling strings upstairs? Would a change in plans have saved all of them? Some of them? Or would it merely have postponed their final fate?

> Incarnacion Martinez, a Puerto Rican laborer living in New York, had a premonition that he would soon be killed. Angel Ortega, whose background was similar to Martinez's but who did not know him, had a feeling he would commit violence with a knife. Neither man knew why or how. The victim-to-be walked into a bar in the early hours of the morning and announced, "I don't have long to live and I don't care who kills me." One of the other patrons was his future murderer, who had taken to carrying a ten-inch bread knife with him, "looking for something to happen." When Martinez left the bar, Ortega was waiting outside, and it was over in a flash. After the stabbing, Ortega told his girlfriend, "I just stabbed a man and I don't even know him."

Why did this happen? Was this man possessed by a force outside of himself that used his body to commit a crime not hatched in the man's own mind? Was this a case of karma, as Hindu philosophers would have it—retribution for something in a former life? Or was it that the other man's number was up, so to speak, and impersonal fate had chosen to dispatch him in this manner?

Certainly, had the personality of the murderer been different, he would not have acted upon his dangerous hunch, and neither would the victim, if he had been a different person. But then, had they both been other people, perhaps their fates would have been altered, too. Consider the ancient story, *Death in Samara*, about a wealthy man who was told that Death was looking for him. So he left his home in Baghdad and journeyed to the distant city of Samara to escape his fate. Unfortunately, when he got to Samara, Death was already there, waiting for him.

In the end, the only satisfactory explanation seems to be that a variety of factors—stationary events caused by forces beyond human scope; individual efforts; reactions and developments following these events; and a little-understood link between past, present, and future—all contribute to what eventually happens to us. For I am convinced that all matters dealing with the unseen world are subject to laws, and are not merely haphazard forays into a colorful world of mysticism.

5

PARANORMAL ABILITY OF THE ORDINARY FIVE SENSES

If you use one of the ordinary five senses—sight, hearing, smell, touch, and taste—for purposes that transcend their usual applications, you are doing something *paranormal*. For instance, if by touching an object you get entire messages or pieces of information that the touch of the object would not ordinarily be likely to give you, then you are having an extrasensory experience even though you are also using one of your ordinary senses.

EXTRAOCULAR VISION

Some individuals have the ability to "read" or to detect colors in the dark with their fingertips. This phenomenon is called extraocular vision.

> Rosa Kuleshova, a twenty-two-year-old Russian woman, was reported to be able to run her fingers over printed text and "read" a newspaper. She could also name colors after touching pieces of colored paper placed in opaque paper envelopes. To prove this, she was tested with a spectroanomaloscope, a device used for testing color vision that generates all colors of the spectrum. Ordinarily, the person being tested puts his or her eye up to the eyepiece. Rosa, however, was blindfolded, and she put her fingertip to the eyepiece. She then correctly named all the colors presented to her for identification.

The Parapsychology Foundation has conducted various

investigations that have yielded additional data and identified a number of people with this ability. Those found to have
"finger vision" were otherwise normal people who merely
had this additional gift, an extension of ordinary sensitivity.

If colors are a form of radiation—and most scientists will
agree that they are—then there really is nothing so terribly
remarkable about a person being able to register color or other
radiation by touch. After all, many human beings can register
psychic radiation, which is a far more complex matter.

Unusual usage of the ordinary sensory organs is frequently found among those who are deprived of one of their senses, whether by nature or by accident. It is common knowledge that blind people often develop extremely acute senses
of hearing or touch, for instance, and manage to perform
some of the functions formerly done by means of the sight
organs with the other senses. Learning to do this normally
takes years, and the degree of alternate perception varies with
the individual. However, it may be possible to accelerate the
process. There is a Thai physician, Dr. Vichit Sukhakarn, who
has used hypnosis to teach blind people how to see with their
"inner eyes."

There is much evidence in addition to Dr. Sukhakarn's
work to suggest that there is a duplicate set of eyes in the
human makeup, just as there are duplicate organs for other
functions. Since the etheric body is a complete duplicate of
the physical body (although more sensitive than the physical
body), it stands to reason that it contains eyes as well.
According to Dr. Sukhakarn, certain areas of the head are
highly sensitive to light rays when a person is hypnotized to
so receive sight impressions. The left cheek is particularly
sensitive to light rays. Accordingly, Dr. Sukhakarn instructs
his pupils to "see" from that area. This technique works, and
the doctor has been able to help many blind people to regain
consciousness of the sight world.

In general, extrasensory perception tends to be greater
when ordinary sensory stimuli are shut out. This conviction is
behind the practice of yogic meditation, and is also the under-
lying idea of the "witch's cradle," a device used by would-be
occult practitioners over the centuries. This is nothing more

than a kind of straitjacket that deprives the user of all movement, no matter how small, and all sight and hearing, thus suspending him or her in a limbo of total quietness that allows the inner self to develop its powers freely.

There are also some stage magicians and mentalists who, although not blind, have genuine extraocular vision. A case in point was a Canadian woman known as "Lady Rhoda" Koren, who demonstrated her strange powers by driving blindfolded through the crowded streets of Ottawa one Monday morning. She supposedly discovered her "x-ray vision" when she was performing on a late-night television show as a magician, and a hood was placed over her head.

How does this work? Are those who can see through blindfolds merely perpetrating a fraud, or do they have extra-sensitive eyes? I think neither explanation will fit. Some of those who truly demonstrated the ability to see while blindfolded were so closely watched that fraud was out of the question. And I do not think their eyes were any better than those of other people. However, they seemed to have a greater ability to use their counterpart eyes—their etheric eyes—and it was with that sight that they were able to perform the seemingly impossible. Lady Rhoda said that her unusual powers of sight existed only if her eyes were *closed*. The moment she opened them, her x-ray vision was gone. This would fit my view, since shutting your eyes to all light (or as much as you are able to) is a form of closing out outside stimuli, and thus setting into motion psychic perception operating directly from the etheric, inner body—from the inside out, as it were.

Individuals who have the capacity of extraocular vision apparently have highly sensitive nerve endings in other parts of their bodies, and perceive through them. If we understand that objects, as well as living beings, all give off a form of radiation, then we can see that such reading is accomplished by making use of and interpreting this signal—much as a radio receiver intercepts, and then transforms into words, the signals emanating from a distant radio transmitter. It stands to reason that some of the most sensitive areas of the body are where most of the nerve endings are—that is, the fingertips, toes, face, and head.

PSYCHOMETRY

One of the more common forms of extrasensory perception is called psychometry, or "measuring with your psychic sense" the emanations from another person. This too is an example of using an ordinary sense to get information not normally available through that sense.

Impressions gained through psychometry can deal with the past, present, or future. Indeed, as we have seen, from the psychic point of view, all three time states are really one continuous state. The barriers between a past that is gone forever, a present that is now, and a future that is not yet, do not exist in the psychic realm, which is why a psychically gifted person can see clearly that which ordinarily is veiled.

Psychometry is so common that I am inclined to accept it as a vestigial form of intuition, originally built into us as a natural extension of our five senses but lost through civilization and lack of use. I myself have developed a mild degree of it over the years without looking for it. In experimenting with this gift on hundreds of occasions with carefully selected strangers, I have found that my accuracy rate has been much higher than mere chance would account for.

Sometimes the mere sight of a stranger can bring forth a reaction in a sensitive person. Such reactions, purely emotional and illogical as they are, often turn out to be entirely correct. Artistic and highly developed persons may form deeper or more rapid impressions, but almost all normal individuals have had such impressions at one time or another. This type of hunch is directly related to intuition and, thus, to premonition. It is merely a more rudimentary form of the same sense.

People who have true psychometric ability, however, usually must touch an object belonging to the person they wish to explore. This object may be anything from a watch or pocket comb to a letter or lock of hair. It is best not to use an antique or an object that has been carried on more than one person's body for any length of time. The best object is one that the owner personally obtained and that he or she has not lent to anyone else. A ring or anything else worn directly on the body is ideal. The psychometrist touches this object, relaxes a little, and then, gradually, enters the atmosphere of the person being read.

Psychometry works best when there is a rapport between reader and subject. However, for obvious reasons, it is desirable that the reader know little or nothing about the person who is the subject of the reading beforehand (he or she may ask after the reading is completed whether the material obtained was correct or not).

How can a "dead" object, made by man, have the power to transmit information about its owner? On the surface, it sounds absurd. But it really is quite logical. We are living electromagnetic entities. Part of ourselves is forever flowing out from us in the form of radiation. This small leakage of energy is similar to the radiation given off by other living things, or even by such inorganic matter as stars or radioactive materials. This radiation that is forever flowing from the owner of an object coats the object with an invisible, but not immaterial, film of magnetic energy. This small part of the owner clings to the object forever, unless and until it is superseded by the outflow of a new owner, whose magnetic radiation then covers up the previous layer clinging to the object.

But how does it follow that a sensitive person can read actual events or facts from an object, even if it is covered with human radiation? After all, radiation is impersonal—merely a collection of small particles of energy traveling at a set rate of speed. The answer to this lies in the nature of humanity itself. A human being is essentially a unique electromagnetic field, consisting of pure energy, temporarily housed in a denser layer of matter called the physical body. This field is capable of being impressed with emotional memories that are stored in it forever, much as a computer is able to store information and give it back on command.

Your experiences alter your electromagnetic field—which is your personality, uniquely different for each and every human being—and part of this "adjusted" field flows out continually. Some of it covers the various objects you have on your person. When a psychometrist gives a reading, he or she comes in contact with the flux—the radiation—from such an object, and gets impulses from it that he or she is able to put into words or word-pictures via his or her own psychic apparatus. Psychometrically gained impressions are always emotionally tinged. Purely logical material does not seem to survive. The outbursts of emotional energy that accompany traumatic events furnish the raw material that coats objects, people, or places, and that contains the memory banks of the events themselves.

In touching an object, person, or being that was in the immediate vicinity of an event, we can replay the event much as a tape player replays a prerecorded audiotape. The events themselves do not possess any active life; the reproduction is faithful, but subject to the limitations of the transmission and the personality traits of the receiver. Therefore, a psychometrically transmitted message may contain part or all of the original event; it may come through correctly or partially correctly; and it may be a mixture of event and personal interpretation—since, after all, the receiver is human and not a machine.

So in touching an object coated with its owner's radiation, the sensitive person can partake of the owner's emotional experiences. It is easy to see that past or even present emotional stimuli, already embedded in the subject's personality field, can be read in this manner. But what about events that have not yet taken place?

In many years of investigation, I have found that the majority of material psychometrists obtain pertains to the past and present. However, there is also an appreciable amount of information obtained through psychometry that deals with future events and that later proves to be true.

Some people have suggested that psychometric impressions of the future only appear to come true because the subjects of the readings are so influenced by the psychometrist's impressions that they *make* them come true. But to suggest that the mere prediction of future events or actions makes an individual undertake them does not answer the question at all. Most of the events investigated are of the kind that the subject could not possibly influence, either consciously or unconsciously. For instance, if a psychometrist touches a piece of paper on which the subject has scribbled a few non-committal words, and then goes on to tell the subject that he sees her carrying a briefcase, she will not, if she has any sense, rush out and buy a briefcase just to make the prediction come true. A few years ago a New York psychometrist said just that to a woman from Australia he had never met before (and never met again, for that matter). At the time, she was a retired musical comedy dancer, passing through New York with her daughter on her way to Europe. Long after this visit she developed an interest in the law, and she is now indeed carrying a briefcase as a practicing trial lawyer.

When a psychometrist foresees future events that cannot be picked up from the unconscious of the subject or deduced in any logical way from his or her appearance, then we must assume that a person's electromagnetic field—his or her personality—can, in some unknown way, also store impulses pointing to the future without the individual being aware of them.

Although the majority of professional mediums practicing their skills in the United States consider themselves clairvoyants, many of them are really psychometrists. They require a few words written on a piece of paper or a personal object that has been touched by the subject to get their impressions. The proof of the pudding, of course, is in the accuracy of the information. This is especially important when dealing with future events, as the number of false or partially false predictions from psychometry outweigh the true ones. But even a share of 20 percent of true readings is far in excess of the percentage that might be explained by guesswork, coincidence (if there is such a thing), or other such factors.

Where does that leave you, the average person interested in psychometry? Try it. For one thing, it is absolutely safe. Nobody, but nobody, ever got hurt by holding an object and trying to get impressions of a psychic nature from it. Having done an occasional bit of psychometry myself and found myself startled when my readings proved accurate, I can describe the sensations that go with such an attempt from firsthand experience.

I touch the object, relax, and wait. If I am successful, pictures, words, and names will literally spring to mind in rapid succession. Sometimes I will get entire sentences, sometimes only vague impressions of things—but they occur far more quickly than I would be able to formulate them as my own thoughts. Also, I have found that there is a difference between my own thoughts and those that flow into me from an object I am holding. That is, my own thoughts are put together "left to right," word by word, and continue to ramble on. Genuine psychometric impressions, on the other hand, come to me "right to left," flowing toward me already constructed. The whole thought comes as one flash—far more quickly and more completely than my own mind could fabricate it.

I advise against using antiques or objects that may have been used in violence, especially if you are a true medium and not merely a casual psychometrist. I once brought a medium a carefully wrapped metallic object to psychometrize without telling her what it was. Turning out the lights so that the medium could not obtain visual impressions from it, I quickly gave it to her. With a shriek, she first clutched and then threw it from her. I asked her what was the matter, and she replied, "Terrible. . . . They use it to kill people. . . stab victims. . . sacrifice. . . in the mountains. . . snow country." The object, as it happened, was a Tibetan *dorje*—a ceremonial object, consisting of a scepter ending in a sharp dagger, that is used in sacrificial rites.

Among the controlled experiments with psychometry that have been undertaken was one by Dr. Karlis Osis (now research director of the American Society of Psychic Research, but then in the same capacity with the Parapsychology Foundation). This consisted of a series of tests that involved placing various objects in similar cardboard boxes, identified only by code numbers on the outside.

These objects were then turned over to the experimenter by the owners of the objects. The experimenter in turn—to avoid any conscious or unconscious picking up of impressions from the owners—invited a group of people not connected with the objects to be tested as proxy sitters—that is, substitutes for the actual owners of the objects who would thus be unaware of their nature. These proxy sitters then selected certain objects at random. The medium being tested was shown in and started to read the still-boxed objects. Only after the experiment was completed were the objects revealed and their nature—and the nature of their owners—compared to the information supplied psychically.

RADIESTHESIA

A very old and highly respected branch of extrasensory activity that relies on physical organs for readings that they would ordinarily not give is *radiesthesia*—better known as "dowsing" or "water-witching." A person with this talent—really a form of psychic ability, too—can discover the presence of water or metals underground merely by holding a forked stick in his or her hands. Instantly, the dowsing rod moves as if pulled by magnetic forces in the ground. The wood itself has no powers, but when the sensitive picks it up, he or she becomes a human water detector. Ancient civilizations referred to this type of activity as using a "divining rod."

Some people prefer to employ a pendulum—a heavy object at the end of a piece of string—to obtain similar results. In either case, the instrument itself is nothing without the user— that is, it is merely an indicator of a person's psychic ability to locate hidden magnetic fields, geophysical disturbances, and other forms of soil radiation.

A geologist and professor in Halle, Germany, evaluated 450 university students and their reactions over geophysical disturbances commonly detected by sensitive dowsers. He found that about 10 percent of all students were able to obtain a reaction with a dowsing rod, and that all of them showed increased blood pressure and a higher pulse rate over reaction zones. This should not be surprising. At its core, all of life is essential radiation, or the continued disintegration of small particles at a high rate of speed.

We know that many illnesses can be traced not to some elusive bug, but to continued exposure to earth radiation. Certain types of cancer, for instance, can have that origin. We know also that the position of a bed can influence the soundness of sleep; if by chance you sleep over a disturbed area, the radiation will penetrate into your unconscious mind and register there. Even as we search the skies and the far corners of outer space, we are duty-bound to investigate inner space—ourselves—and the planet we inhabit. The truth is that we know precious little about the nature of our earth, not even what it consists of all the way down. The nature of force fields that exist in the earth is likewise unknown; even less do we understand the responses of plants, animals, or the human body to these force fields.

I have no doubt that there are hundreds of individuals throughout the world with the ability to "read" the signs emanating from the earth, from inanimate objects, and from other living beings. There is nothing miraculous about it. The extension of the abilities of the ordinary human senses is merely part of the ever-widening quest into the nature of the psychic.

6

OUT-OF-BODY EXPERIENCES AND BILOCATION

The phenomena of out-of-body experiences and bilocation prove that we can (and sometimes do) function fully without the physical body. This is because there is within each of us a secondary body—variously called the etheric body, aura, or soul—that is the true vehicle of the self. The movement of this inner body, and all communications by and with it, are part of the dimension we call the astral, the etheric, or the psychic.

According to theosophy (a branch of religious philosophy devoted to studying the nature of the soul) and, to a lesser degree, ancient Egyptian religion, a human being has five bodies, of which the astral body is but one. In this system, the astral world is the second lowest of seven worlds, and is characterized by emotions, desires, and passions. This, of course, is a philosophical concept, and you may choose to believe it or not. I myself choose to relate to the astral world as merely the "other side of life." (*See* Psychic Ability and the "Other Side of Life," page 68.) By doing so, I may be simplifying things, but it seems to me that proving the existence of one nonphysical sphere is quite enough for parapsychologists at this stage of the game. If there are other, finer layers within that sphere—and I do not doubt in the least that there may be—let us leave discussions of that for a time when the very existence of the nonphysical world is no longer subject to such great doubt, especially among scientists.

Psychic Ability and
the "Other Side of Life"

Many people readily accept the reality of extrasensory perception, but strenuously object to the possibility that the human personality may survive beyond physical death. After all, psychic
phenomena such as telepathy or psychometry, or even clairvoyance and the ability to look into the future, can be explained
without the need to assume a world beyond this one. These
phenomena may defy commonly accepted laws of cause and
effect, but they do not imply the existence of a completely different order of things, one that would necessitate a radical
rethinking of one's philosophy.

When we come to the question of the "other side," an entire
realm apart from the physical one we wake up to every day,
we are opening a Pandora's box. Indeed, if there is such a
thing, then our concepts of life and what it means to be human
need to be greatly modified.

Yet there is reason to believe that there is indeed such a
dimension, based on abundant evidence from the out-of-body
experiences of many individuals here on earth and also on per-
suasive evidence of communications received from those who
inhabit the other side. It is common to refer to these personalities as the dead, but it is more accurate to describe them as discarnate—that is, no longer living *in the physical world*—for reasons that shall shortly become apparent.

The discarnate communicate with the living in haphazard
and surprising ways. The sudden apparition, the sound of a
voice in an empty room, visits from long-dead relatives and
friends, farewell greetings at the time of passing—all these
phenomena are very common. Communications between the
living and the dead, whether initiated by the dead or by the
living, use extrasensory perception to make themselves felt.
Only if the recipient of such a communication has sufficient
psychic ability to perceive the emanations sent out from the
nonphysical world can his or her conscious mind register the
information. An emergency, an emotional necessity, or any
kind of urgency will make the impact much stronger, of course,

as it does in the case of telepathic communication between living persons.

Some people shrug off evidence of communication from the "other side" as hallucinations due to some type of emotional or psychological malfunction in the observer. While this may be possible in a number of cases—for instance, when a bereaved individual claims to have been contacted by a recently deceased loved one—it certainly could not explain the many "surprise visits" by dead individuals to people who did not know they had passed on, or even to people who never knew them at all. For example, you may have had the experience of staying at someone else's house and being surprised by the apparition of a dead individual about whom you know nothing, but who, you later learn, was the very image of a person formerly associated with the house. Many people have reported the appearance of a dear one at the same time that person is dying or has just died—without, of course, knowing at the time that this was happening. The discarnate also can communicate information by means of vocal phenomena. People who have experienced such contact run the gamut of professions, ages, and national and educational backgrounds.

That there is another dimension close to this one in which we live I do not doubt in the least. That dimension seems essentially to be a thought world, in which everything consists of specific electromagnetic fields containing memories and emotional stimuli that can be identified with individuals formerly alive in physical bodies. For all practical purposes, then, we may theorize that the dead are nothing more than the inner selves of living people—the same type of astral, or etheric, selves that may engage in astral travel. The chief difference seems to be that the etheric body of a discarnate person no longer has to carry the weight of the outer layer that is the physical body. Keep in mind that energy and mass are of one kind, and differ only in density, in form; whether energy manifests itself as "energy" or as "mass," as we understand the terms, depends on factors such as temperature, pressure, and speed. Compare this, if you will, to water. It can take the form of ice or steam, depending on temperature and pressure, but it is still water. The physical body (the outer layer of the personality) is subject to the influences of a three-dimensional physical world, and responds accordingly. The inner layer—the etheric or inner, duplicate body within each of us—responds only to the mind and the world of mind, which I call the Other Side of Life.

In the other dimension, the mind can create anything it wishes, and anything so created is manifested as solid, "three-dimensional" reality until or unless the mind that created it decides to change it or dissolve it again. If such mind creations are brought into the physical world, they appear two-dimensional. If these mind creations—or apparitions or what have you—are to appear fully three-dimensional in the three-dimensional physical world, they have to be reinforced with matter (compressed energy) from a living person or persons. The resulting three-dimensional "matter" is ectoplasm, which is cold and waxy to the touch but appears to the eye to be fully lifelike and three-dimensional.

Whether they are materialistically or religiously inclined, people almost always respond to the possibility of communication from another dimension with doubt, if not fear. Only a small minority are prepared to consider such occurrences as natural. As with most psychic phenomena, receiving such communications cannot be planned or forced. All you can hope for is to be a good channel—relaxed in body, mind, and spirit, and accepting of the reality of such communications and all they imply. There is no way to communicate with the Other Side of Life except through psychic channels. Only thought forms can break through the barrier separating the two worlds. The stronger your psychic ability and the more disciplined your application of it, the more likely it is that you may have contact with those who have gone on to the nonphysical world.

The astral dimension is made up of very fine particles. It is certainly not intangible. The etheric body, which represents the true human personality, is made up of the same type of substance, and it is able to exist freely in the etheric dimension after the death of the physical body. As long as a person is alive in the physical world, his or her astral body remains attached to its physical counterpart by a thin connecting link called the *silver cord,* a kind of cable through which impulses go back and forth. If the cord is severed, physical death results. At the time of physical death, the cord is indeed severed and the astral body floats freely outward into the next dimension.

OUT-OF-BODY EXPERIENCES

The out-of-body experience is also known as astral projection, because it represents the projection of the inner layer of the body—the astral or etheric body—into the astral world without hurting the physical body. When the inner body is projected outward into the world outside the physical body, it gains a degree of freedom that it does not enjoy while encased in the physical body. Today, however, we tend to use the more accurate term *out-of-body experience.* The reason that this is a more accurate term is that projection as such — that is to say, a willful outward movement out of the physical body—is rarely the means by which the phenomenon occurs. Rather, it takes the form of a feeling of dissociation between the physical and the etheric bodies—a floating sensation during which the inner self seems to be leaving its physical counterpart and traveling away from it. The movement toward the outside is by no means rapid or projection-like. In most cases, it is a slow, gradual disengagement. Occasionally there are dramatic instances in which astral projection occurs spontaneously and rather suddenly. But such cases usually involve some form of shock or induced trauma, such as surgery, anesthesia, sudden grief, sudden joy, or overwhelming fatigue.

Out-of-body experiences can be divided roughly into two categories: spontaneous cases, in which they occur without being induced in any way and are usually a surprise; and experimental cases, in which the state of dissociation is deliberately induced by various means. The defining issue in astral projection, whether voluntary or involuntary, is the question of whether the traveler makes an impact on the other end of the line, so to speak. If the travel is observed, preferably in some detail, by the recipient of the projection, and if that information is made available only after the event itself, it constitutes a valuable piece of evidence for the reality of this particular psychic phenomenon.

Spontaneous Out-of-Body Experiences

Astral travel is so common an experience that the files of the American Society for Psychical Research (the oldest research society in the field) are bulging with this type of report. The loosening of the bond between the physical and the etheric bodies can occur as a result of a number of factors, chiefly the state of relaxation experienced just before the onset of sleep or just before awakening.

It would appear that the physical body and the inner, etheric body are not always as solidly intertwined as you might think. When thoughts wander and a person's attention drifts, the inner body, containing the true personality, may slip out involuntarily—accidentally as it were—and wander about, leading a life of its own unencumbered by the controlling influence of the conscious mind. It may be attracted to strange scenes or it might find itself compelled to visit well-known places or persons.

A Japanese-American woman, Mrs. Y., lived in New York and had a sister in California. One day, Mrs. Y. found herself projected through space from her New York home to her sister's place on the West Coast. She had not been there for many years, and no longer really knew what it looked like (considerable alterations had taken place about the house since she had last visited). As she swooped down onto her sister's home, Mrs. Y. noticed the changes in the house and saw her sister, wearing a green dress, standing on the front lawn. She tried to attract her sister's attention but was unable to do so. Worried about her unusual state of being—that is, floating above the ground and seemingly being unable to be observed—Mrs. Y. became anxious. That moment she found herself yanked back to her New York home, where she was lying in bed. As she returned to her own body, she experienced a sensation of falling from a great height. The following day, Mrs. Y. contacted her sister, telling her what she had seen. To Mrs. Y.'s surprise, her sister confirmed everything she had seen during her astral flight.

The sensation of spinning down from a great height accompanies most, if not all, returns from astral travel. It represents a reverse reaction to the slowing down in speed of the etheric body as it reaches the physical body and prepares to reenter it, much as you might lurch forward in a fast-moving vehicle that stops suddenly. Many people complain of dreams in which they fall from great heights only to awaken to a sensation of a dizzying fall and resulting anxiety. The majority of such experiences are probably due to astral travel, but unlike Mrs. Y., most people do not remember the entire experience.

Sometimes astral travel involves changes of time as well as location.

Ruth Knuths, a legal secretary and former teacher, was living in San Diego, California, having moved there from Del Rio, Texas. She was riding to work on a streetcar, with nothing in particular on her mind. It was eight o'clock in the morning. Suddenly, she found herself standing on the front porch of her good friend Jo Comstock's house back in Del Rio. People were driving up and parking their cars at the edge of the unfenced yard. They were coming to express their sympathy on the death of Jo's mother. (The funeral was to be that afternoon.) Ruth knew that Jo was inside the house, although she did not see her, and she stood and greeted the arriving friends for her. Then, as suddenly as she had gone to Del Rio, Ruth was back in the streetcar, still two or three blocks away from her stop.

Two weeks later, Ruth learned that Jo's mother had suffered a stroke the same day that Ruth had had her vision. The stroke had occurred at about ten o'clock in the morning, and Jo had been notified at ten-thirty. Jo said she had badly wished that Ruth had been there with her. Allowing for the time difference between San Diego and Del Rio—two hours—Ruth calculated that she had had the experience on the streetcar at the very time Jo's mother had had the stroke, but that the vision was projected ahead of that by two days, to the day of the funeral.

Sometimes it is not clear to the traveler whether he or she has had a vision of events at a distance or actually traveled to them.

Just before falling asleep, Richard Smith, a self-employed landscape service contractor in his thirties, found himself floating through the air across the country to his wife's parents' home in Michigan. He moved about the house and watched his father-in-law as he read the newspaper, moved through the rooms, and drank a cup of coffee. Richard could not find his mother-in-law in the house, however. She apparently was out working. Richard felt he was floating at a point near the ceiling and looking down. His father-in-law happened to look up from his coffee and seemed to be frightened. He looked all around the room in a state of great uneasiness, as if he could sense someone in the room. Richard left, as he did not wish to frighten his wife's father by his presence. Richard says he has had psychic experiences since childhood and seems to be able to travel anywhere, almost at will, as long as the conditions are right.

The majority of spontaneous out-of-body experiences take place during sleep. Indeed, they constitute one of the four types of dream states described by individuals upon awakening (more about dream states in Chapter 9). The difference between out-of-body experiences during sleep and ordinary dreams is quite marked. We frequently remember ordinary dreams only in part, if at all, and even if we remember them upon awakening, they are quickly forgotten. Out-of-body experiences, on the other hand, are remembered clearly and in every detail, and the memory persists for days. They are to ordinary dreams what a color slide is to an old black-and-white print.

It stands to reason that the majority of out-of-body experiences occur during sleep, when the bonds between the conscious and unconscious minds are relaxed. Occasionally, people have out-of-body experiences while fully awake, not only when resting or sitting down, but even while driving a car or walking. These experiences tend to be of very short duration, fortunately, and I know of no instance in which accidents have occurred due to this momentary displacement. There seems to be some sort of superior law watching over individuals with this particular gift, making sure that they do not suffer because of it.

Induced Out-of-Body Experiences

Induced astral projection is a subject that has fascinated researchers almost from the start of modern parapsychology. Because such experiments are repeatable and offer satisfactory control conditions, they are frequently used to demonstrate the presence of psychic capabilities in people. Certainly it is more possible to induce out-of-body travel than any other form of psychic experience. It is the one type of psychic phenomenon that does not require true emotional motivation to succeed. The adventure and excitement of leaving one's body, even if temporarily, seem to be sufficient.

Some years ago, I was working with a group of students headquartered at the New York City offices of the Association for Research and Enlightenment (ARE), better known as the Cayce Foundation (it was founded by the late medium Edgar Cayce and devotes itself to the study of his work). We had at our disposal a young man named Stanley, who was capable of deliberate astral projection. In one experiment, a research team set up controlled conditions in an apartment on East 82nd Street, while another research team met at the ARE headquarters on West 16th Street. The 82nd Street team decided to use as "markers" a book opened to a certain page and a flower in a vase. In the ARE offices, Stanley was placed in a light hypnotic trance and directed to visit the 82nd Street apartment. While there, if possible, he was to make his presence known to the observers, and upon awakening, he was to report everything he had observed.

The entire experiment took no more than half an hour. When it was completed, Stanley woke up, rubbed his eyes, and reported that shortly after he had projected himself outward from his physical body, he had found himself floating through the apartment on 82nd Street. He said that he had gone to the kitchen of the apartment, which he found bathed in blue-white light. At all times, he said, he had had the sensation of being slightly above the floor, floating rather than actually walking upon it. He described the observers and also the flower and the book. However, he said, he had not been able to arouse the observers to acknowledge his presence, even though he had tried to touch them. His hand seemed to go right through them, and he was unable to make his presence known to them.

DEMONSTRATING THE VALIDITY OF OUT-OF-BODY EXPERIENCES

I know of no other field of scientific inquiry where so little progress is apparent on the surface as in parapsychology. I do not mean to say that progress is not being made—far from it—but in terms of public knowledge, very little is being disclosed today that was not already disclosed long ago. This may be due to the fact that the climate for this type of research was more favorable twenty or thirty years ago than it seems to be today. First of all, there were more funds available, but beyond this, I have noticed a certain timidity on the part of some academic parapsychologists for which there is neither need nor explanation. In any case, the amount of material that has been obtained through the proper observation of spontaneous psychic phenomena is tremendous and deserves a wider circulation in every sense of the term.

On the other hand, material published even twenty or thirty years ago is still perfectly valid. Repeated experiments have confirmed earlier findings, and continue to confirm them today. Thus, what more recent works on out-of-body experiences have said confirm the findings of the late Dr. Hornell Hart, who, as a professor at Duke University, was a close collaborator of Dr. Joseph Rhine, the legendary founder and head of Duke's parapsychology laboratory. Later, Hart became chairman of the Committee on Spontaneous Cases of the American Society for Psychical Research. He put together a summation of his intensive research into out-of-body experiences. Entitled "ESP Projection: Spontaneous Cases and Repeatable Experi-ments," this classic report covered a total of 288 cases of purported out-of-body experiences. Of these, 99 were found to be convincing and useful for the project. These cases were then divided into five types, the first three involving projections induced experimentally and the other two consisting of spontaneous out-of-body experiences:

1. Hypnotically induced projections (20 cases).

2. Intentional projection of one's own apparition by concentration (15 cases).

3. Self-projection by more elaborate methods (12 cases).

4. Spontaneous apparitions of the living, corresponding with dreams or other concentration of attention by the appearers (30 cases).

5. Other spontaneous cases (22 cases).

Based on this analysis, Hart concluded, "The fifteen reported successes in projecting one's own apparition plus the thirty spontaneous cases of apparitions of living persons coinciding with dreams or other directions of attention by the appearer suggest that such experiments are at least occasionally repeatable."

One of the arguments sometimes put forth against the reality of astral travel—both by parapsychologists and by those outside the field—is that the phenomenon can be explained as simple telepathy, clairvoyance, or precognition. According to Hart, however, only out-of-body experience provided a framework into which all of the 99 cases he studied would fit. Moreover, he said, while astral projection does involve telepathy, clairvoyance, and precognition, simple telepathy and clairvoyance do not involve projection of viewpoint—perceiving from and being perceived in positions outside of the physical body—as out-of-body experiences do.

In his summation of the investigation, Hart listed the following conclusions:

- Out-of-body experiences are frequent.
- Out-of-body experiences may be genuine.
- Out-of-body experiences can be produced experimentally.

Further, pilot studies conducted at Duke University showed that, in representative samples of students, precognitive dreams were reported by 36 percent; perception of apparitions by about 10 percent; and out-of-body experiences by 33 percent.

TAPPING YOUR POTENTIAL FOR OUT-OF-BODY EXPERIENCES

Because the ability to have out-of-body experiences is comparatively common, and because they can sometimes be intentionally induced, experiments with astral projection may be more likely to succeed than deliberate attempts at other types of psychic experiences. People who have a tendency to sleepwalk are more likely than others to have out-of-body experiences. These are usually people with strong psychic tendencies, very imaginative and very easily influenced. Hardheaded, businesslike, or basically suspicious individuals generally make poor astral travelers. This is not to say that imagination is necessary for out-of-body experiences to succeed. Nor should one assume that imaginary experiences are at the root of astral travel. Far from it; these experiences are quite real in every sense of the word. But it is true that a tendency toward visualization—a tendency toward dreaming, perhaps—helps to permit the disengagement of the astral body from its physical counterpart.

Whether you are particularly suited to astral travel by nature, or simply intrigued by the possibility and want to try it, the technique remains the same. It is best done at an hour of the day when you are reasonably relaxed, possibly physically tired. The room in which the experiment is to take place must be quiet, not too brightly lit, and neither too warm nor too cold. Above all, there should be little noise or other distraction.

Stretch out on a couch or bed, close your eyes, and suggest to yourself the loosening of the bonds between your conscious and unconscious minds. Picture yourself floating up from your body toward the ceiling. Inevitably, this self-suggestion will lead to a sense of giddiness or lightheadedness. Eventually, you will feel your limbs becoming lighter, and you may not even feel them at all after awhile. As the experiment continues, you will feel yourself rising, or rather have a sensation of weightlessness. At this point, the disengagement from your physical body may begin. Your inner self may leave your physical body through the upper solar plexus, the top of the head, or the stomach area.

Some experimenters have described a sensation of slowly rising straight up to the ceiling of the room, then stopping and looking down at their sleeping bodies. Others have found themselves in the corner of the room, somewhat frightened by it all, looking back upon their sleeping counterparts. At all times, the personality and the seat of ego remain in the astral body. The sleeping physical body continues to breathe regularly and maintain its functions as if the personality of the astral traveler were still inside it. This is made possible by the connecting silver cord, which, though invisible to the outside world, serves as a link between the two bodies.

It is important to realize that the moment of disengagement is by no means a moment of panic or confusion. An astral traveler thinks clearly, perhaps more clearly than when in the physical body. Once disengagement has taken place, you will be capable of directing yourself toward whatever goal you have chosen. You may, at your discretion, choose to wander about or simply float out the window to observe the world around you.

In this state, you are able to partake of two worlds: the physical world, which you have just left temporarily, and the nonphysical world, in which those we call the dead lead their continued existence. Thus, you may well find yourself face to face with friends or relatives who have passed on, or with strangers who seem quite clearly no longer in the physical life. From the astral traveler's point of view, there is no difference between the living and the dead; both seem three-dimensional and there is no feeling of transparency or a two-dimensional appearance. There is also a total absence of the sense of time. Consequently, you may not realize how long you have been out of your body. You will, however, be capable of ending your excursion by so willing it.

Return to the physical body is accompanied by a sensation of rapid deceleration, experienced as a kind of free-fall—a spinning and, occasionally, unpleasant feeling of having fallen from a great height. This is due to the rapid change in speed between the etheric body and the physical body. The adjustment is comparatively rapid and can therefore be momentarily unpleasant, but it in no way represents danger to either body or mind.

If you initiate your return with a sense of panic, the trip will likely be a rough one, and the awakening in the body may be accompanied by a headache and, possibly, nausea. Consequently, if you experiment with out-of-body experiences, you should not allow yourself to be drawn back too quickly. Rather, you should slowly direct yourself back toward your home, suggesting to yourself that you descend slowly and without undue haste until you find yourself once again in familiar surroundings.

When you arrive above your physical body—hovering above it for a moment, as it were—you will then direct yourself to descend the rest of the way until you "click" into place inside your physical body. This clicking into place is an important part of the return that has been described by nearly all astral travelers. If it does not occur, there may be delayed reactions upon awakening, such as a sense of displacement, confusion, or a dual presence—a feeling that you are in both the astral and the physical world at the same time. If this happens, you may have to be hypnotized and full reintegration of the astral and physical bodies suggested in order for integration to take place. However, this is rarely necessary. Since astral travel requires a fair degree of energy, and since this energy comes from the physical body, you should rest immediately following your return. You should also be sure to drink some liquids to replenish your supply, which will definitely have been reduced during the out-of-body experience.

Induced astral projection should not be undertaken without a helper standing by to arouse you if necessary—for instance, if you have any difficulty coming back into your own body. If this happens, your helper should recall you gently by name, rather than ordering you to return. This is not to say that out-of-body experiences are dangerous. Occasionally, some occultists sound dire warnings of potential possession by an unwanted entity, but I know of absolutely no incident in which an evil entity has taken advantage of the situation and "slipped into" the body of an astral traveler while the owner was out. The danger, if any, of unobserved and uncontrolled astral travel lies in the fact that it is easy to lose track of time, and that you will be unable to report to anyone immediately upon awakening on things you may have encountered. It is therefore best to have another person, preferably a trained researcher, standing by from the beginning to the end of the experiment.

BILOCATION

Bilocation is a phenomenon closely allied with astral travel, but it is a manifestation of its own, with certain distinct features that set it apart from out-of-body experiences as such. In bilocation, a living person is projected to another site and observed there by one or more witnesses while at the same time continuing to function fully and normally in the physical body at the original place. Whereas the physical body of the astral traveler is usually resting in bed—or, in the case of daytime projection, continuing to do whatever the person had been doing, but rather automatically and without consciousness—with bilocation, the individual is fully conscious and continues to act normally, unaware that he or she is being seen at a distance as well.

Near-Death Experiences

Some people—most of them ordinary, average people without the slightest interest in, or knowledge of, psychic matters—have had encounters with the next world without staying in it. Cases of this kind are many, and while the medical profession is still divided about the causes, an increasing number of physicians are convinced that these experiences are not hallucinatory but real—a journey to the dimension next door, so to speak, but with a return ticket for one reason or another.

Most people who have reported near-death experiences have been involved in accidents or undergone surgery, and during a period of unconsciousness—whether from injury, as in the case of an accident or heart attack, or anesthesia, in the case of surgery—became separated from their physical bodies. Some have found themselves able to observe what was being done to them from a new vantage point; others have traveled to the next world in a kind of dream state, and observed conditions there that they remembered upon returning to wakefulness. Not all temporary separations of the physical and etheric self include a visit to the next world. Sometimes, it seems, the liberated self merely hangs around to observe what is being done with the body.

There is a definite pattern in these near-misses, so to speak—the experiences of people who have gone over to the Other Side of Life and then returned. There tends to be a similarity about what such people relate, yet the concurring witnesses have no way of knowing of each other's experiences, have never met, and have not read a common source from which they could draw such material.

Often, for instance, there is a beckoning figure in a flowing robe, sometimes identified as Jesus, sometimes simply as a master. The identification of the figure depends, of course, on the religious or metaphysical attitude of the individual, but the feeling caused by his appearance seems to be universally the same: a sense of peace and complete contentment. Another frequent occurrence is the experience of encountering a dead relative or friend. Sometimes this person appears as if to welcome the newcomer into the next world. It is not uncommon for a dying person to recognize dead relatives in the room, apparently come to help them across the threshold to the Other Side. In a near-death experience, however, the relatives encountered sometimes seem to have come specifically to tell the person that he or she should return to the physical world.

There are many cases on record in which a person has begun to partake of another dimension even while there is still hope for recovery, but the ties between consciousness and body have already begun to loosen. Many cases of this kind occur while a person is being prepared for or is undergoing surgery; it appears that sometimes the anesthetic allows dissociation to occur more easily.

Perhaps the single most common thread in near-death experiences is the feeling of being at peace that seems to follow—a feeling of serenity and contentment and, most notable, a complete absence of the fear of death. Upon their return, these travelers often seem to have undergone profound changes. Their attitudes toward life and death usually change completely, allowing them to live the rest of their lives with a feeling of being more at peace. In addition, in many cases, their inherent psychic ability is fully awakened, and to their amazement, they have become psychic. Apparently exposure to the next dimension, the Other Side, can trigger an increase in psychic ability.

Some people are quick to argue that near-death experiences are nothing more than hallucinations, mental aberrations, or fantasies brought about by situations of extreme stress. I cannot emphasize strongly enough that authentic near-death experiences do not fall into this category. The clarity of the experience, the full memory of it afterwards, and the many parallels between individual experiences reported by different people in widely scattered areas all weigh heavily against the possibility that these experiences are of hallucinatory origin.

Why is it that some people are allowed to glimpse that which lies ahead for them in the next dimension, without actually entering that dimension at the time of the experience? Why do some people get, in effect, an advance look at their own demise? As for the ultimate reason, we do not really know, but it must be that there is some degree of self-determination involved that allows a person to choose to go forward to the next dimension or return to the body. Whatever the reason, though, these witnesses, by disseminating their reports among those in the physical world, put valuable knowledge at our disposal—at least, at the disposal of those who are willing to listen.

Carl Pfau of Savannah, Georgia, was awakened one night by the feeling that he was not alone. Turning over in bed, he saw a good friend, Morton Deutsch, standing by his bedside. "How did you get in here?" he asked, since the door had been securely locked. Morton made no reply, but merely smiled. Then, turning, he walked to the door and disappeared. When Carl asked Morton about it later, Morton told him that at the time of his appearance, he had been sitting in a large, comfortable chair and had just wondered how his friend Carl was doing. Suddenly he had felt himself lifted from the chair and to Carl's bedside. There was a distance of about two miles between their houses.

The following is a case of double bilocation, something that does not happen very often:

Mina Lauterer, a woman who has pronounced psychic talents and is also a very keen observer, was walking down a street in New York's Greenwich Village when she saw a man she knew from Chicago. Surprised to find this person out of his usual element, she crossed the street to greet him. When she tried to reach out toward him, however, he evaporated before her eyes. The incident so disturbed Mina that she contacted the man in Chicago, who told her that he had been in that city at the time she had observed him in New York, but that he had just then been thinking of her.

Whether Mina saw her friend's thought projection or whether a part of him was actually projected to appear in New York is a moot question, and really one of technical definition only. What is more interesting is the fact that *he* saw Mina as he was thinking about her in Chicago.

Bilocation occurs mostly in mentally active people—people whose minds are filled with a variety of ideas, perhaps to the point of distraction. They may be doing one thing while thinking of another at such moments. The majority of cases seem to fall into this category.

Bilocation cannot be artificially induced the way astral projection can, but if you are interested in trying to be seen in two places at once, you may take certain steps to encourage it. For one thing, you should be in a relaxed and comfortable position in a quiet place, whether indoors or outdoors, and allow your thoughts to drift. The more you concentrate, the less likely it is to happen. However, you should be aware that it is very difficult to produce the particular state of dissociation that is conducive to bilocation experiences. Also, in the majority of cases, bilocation is not known to the projecting individual until after it has occurred and been confirmed on the other end.

Bilocation is really nothing but the modern explanation for what European researchers used to call the "double" or, in German, the "Doppelgänger." In accounts of this phenomenon, the incidents were usually seen as having sinister implications, such as impending death. This is not true, of course. Today, the attitude of parapsychologists toward incidents of bilocation and astral projection is almost matter-of-fact, because out-of-body experiences happen frequently, and to people who cannot be accused of hallucinating or worse.

In former days, such happenings were sometimes blamed on "demonic" influences. Such beliefs have deep roots in our culture and are hard to shake. But they have no place in modern parapsychology, which holds that demons and devils exist only in the minds of people who for various reasons find a kind of comfort in believing in them.

7

WHAT EXACTLY IS HYPNOSIS, AND WHAT CAN IT DO?

Although hypnosis is a technique practiced by one person on another, and not in any sense a natural gift or extraordinary facet of personality, it belongs in this book because hypnosis uses some of the elements that are present in natural psychic ability. In both cases, the unconscious portion of the mind is involved.

Hypnosis—or, as it is often wrongly termed, hypnotism— has long been the object of much general fascination. It has also been much abused. I take a dim view of stage hypnotists, for example, who use hypnosis to amuse themselves and others for pay. In the proper hands, hypnosis is a valuable tool of medicine and psychiatry, not a parlor game. It has also increasingly been found to be effective in the exploration of the human mind. In parapsychology and psychic research, it helps psychics to "go under" when required, and is an aid to probing the deeper levels of human consciousness.

THE NATURE OF HYPNOSIS

What exactly is hypnosis? Simply put, it is a state of induced relaxation that eventually progresses into a sleeplike state in which you are consciously removed from the world around you. At the same time, however, you become very close to the hypnotist, whose commands you must obey. As long as you want to be hypnotized to begin with, you will be eager to please the hypnotist, and a close relationship begins. Thus, hypnosis is a way of relaxing and opening up the deepest parts of the mind.

THE USES OF HYPNOSIS

Hypnosis can be used for a variety of purposes. Contrary to the popular misconception, hypnosis is not a way to make a person do things that are against his or her conscious code of behavior (although there are exceptions, such as when a hypnotist draws on a subject's suppressed desires and allows them to be realized). Hypnosis does, however, have a number of important applications, from the medical to the psychological to the psychic.

Medical Treatment

Hypnosis can be an addition to, and often part of, various approaches to health care. It is not a substitute for medical treatment, but can be a valuable assist when properly administered. It can be particularly useful in cases in which drugs cannot be used and some other means of relaxing a patient is needed. For example, many people have been successfully hypnotized to endure the pain of such experiences as childbirth or dental work.

I myself am highly sensitive to the anesthetics normally used by dentists when extracting a tooth. When I needed a tooth removed, and was convinced that the tooth would come out with one good yank—thus involving pain of comparatively short duration—I decided to practice what I preach and refuse the Novocain. Instead, I used autosuggestion, or self-hypnosis, to convince myself that there would be no pain. I visualized a kind of "glass cage" around the affected tooth that would prevent the pain from reaching the nerve center in the brain that would normally register pain from that region. After arriving at the dentist's office, I "relaxed" again for about five minutes, repeating the suggestions to myself in a low voice. With some hesitation, the dentist went to work. I felt a sharp pain but it was bearable—far less than it would have been had I not conditioned myself for it. I did not succeed in eliminating the pain altogether, since I was not truly hypnotized (with a total loss of consciousness), but merely under light suggestion. But I did raise my threshold of pain, and this made the difference between being able to tolerate the pain or not. I walked out of the dentist's office five minutes later without the slightest discomfort.

By itself, hypnosis cannot take the place of general anesthesia if surgery is required. But in cases in which general anesthesia is impossible, a combination of hypnosis and local anesthesia can be sufficient. In addition, hypnosis helps to quell anxiety, which can be more of a problem than actual pain.

Psychological Applications

Hypnosis can be useful for gaining insight into psychological problems. This is because when a person is hypnotized, his or her subconscious mind can speak openly, without the restraining, editing hand of the conscious mind. Thus, the hypnotist can draw out unresolved problems and repressed emotions that may be at the root of difficulties such as anxiety, depression, phobias, and other psychological conditions that can interfere with happiness and everyday life.

It is also possible to use hypnotic suggestion to help improve self-confidence and self-esteem, and to eliminate problem behaviors. For instance, hypnosis can be used to help smokers kick the habit. It is not a magical way to stop smoking, but it *can* help you strengthen your own conscious determination to stop by strengthening your character and helping you to explore any suppressed problems that are the cause of smoking. However, hypnosis will not make you stop smoking if you really want to smoke and have no desire to change. Moreover, if your smoking is an expression of a deeply embedded personality problem, just suppressing the habit might cause problems worse than smoking itself; some other behavior, perhaps even less desirable than smoking, might replace it in your habit pattern. Only a skilled hypnotist can succeed in treating such a case. It requires probing into the personality of the patient and exploring the reasons that he or she smokes before suppressing the habit.

Regression

Regression is a type of psychic experiment that involves the use of hypnosis to take a person, step by step, back into childhood and even beyond the threshold of birth, to earlier lives. It is amazing, but the person who undergoes regression usually does really relive the past, knows exactly what it was like, and even recalls names and other information he or she no longer consciously remembers.

The mind, operating through the brain, is such a marvelous instrument that it never loses anything that is put into it. Things may be subdued, repressed, put into a far-off corners, yes—but forgotten, no. In regression, the hypnotist's command brings out information from those hidden corners and the subject (the person under hypnosis) lives the moment over again; he or she acts, responds, and talks just as if the time were now and the people he or she once associated with were right there in the room again.

Before the classic Morey Bernstein work, *Search for Bridey Murphy,* was published in the 1950s, very few people outside the psychiatric laboratory had ever even heard of regression. Today, it is almost a parlor game—a development I thoroughly disapprove of. What Bernstein did was to take a hypnotized subject, step by step, back into childhood and then back beyond birth. In the process, he succeeded in finding an entirely new personality from an earlier lifetime. This created quite a stir in the scientific community and among the public generally, and there were numerous attempts to discredit Bernstein's work as a a hoax. The dickens it was. (I know because I was there from the start.) Moreover, the case of

Bridey Murphy was not unique by any means. Long before, in Stockholm, a Swedish physician had done the same thing—that is, found evidence for an earlier existence in various subjects.

In my own experience, people I have hypnotized do not know the names or circumstances they speak of under hypnosis while conscious in today's world; yet, on researching the material, I have found that the information they gave was correct. In one case, I recall that the subject gave the names of two school chums at age ten, using their nicknames. This was later confirmed. In other cases, street addresses long receded into the darkest recesses of the mind proved to be correct for the time period stated.

In several cases, I have found another personality on my hands.

> Jeane Williams, a Broadway dancer, came to me for regression. Although her formal schooling had ended in the third year of high school, she was a bright and worldly wise young woman with a keen curiosity about and interest in the occult. When I took her beyond the birth moment, she suddenly became an East Indian living in a house that she was able to describe in great detail. She also used words that I was later able to identify as Hindi. Since Jeane had little education, had never been abroad, and did not have any unusual linguistic talent, this could not be dismissed as merely a matter of picking up knowledge from books or other sources.

Experiments with hypnotic regression should always be undertaken under the supervision of a professional hypnotist trained in parapsychology. It is best if the hypnotist suggests to the subject that any past memory retrieved in this way will not be retained upon awakening. This helps to avoid any traumatic residue. Thus, the only information about the past made available is that which the hypnotized subject brings while in the hypnotized state. Further, hypnotic regression is more concerned with personal experiences in past lives rather than with historical facts, so its usefulness in purely past-oriented research is limited.

HOW IS HYPNOSIS DONE?

A well-known psychiatrist once described words as "triggers to action." That is, the proper words can make people take actions. In fact, words can do all sorts of things. For instance, words of praise can make you work harder, run faster, or behave in a jollier way. A word of criticism can do the opposite. Whether or not we consciously believe the words, they do their work. Indeed, words—which are outward expressions of thoughts—are the key to our behavior. Hypnosis makes careful use of the right words, properly selected to reduce the subject's own willpower, said in just the right rhythmic pattern to encourage the sleep centers in the mind.

Different hypnotists use different methods to help their subjects achieve the hypnotic state. Some like to have their subjects concentrate on shining objects, and thus speed withdrawal from the surrounding world. Candles or swinging pendulums have also been used. These devices can heighten the effect, but I prefer to use words only.

To begin with, I make sure that a person seeking hypnosis has come to me not out of idle curiosity but because a genuine need exists. The need may be personal and involve a problem, such as smoking, or it may be a serious interest in researching such phenomena as psychic trance, regression, and other forms of probing human consciousness. I always try to assist those in need of personal help, within the framework of existing medical convention; that is, if a person has been through medical treatment and/or conventional psychiatry and not been helped, I might offer to try hypnosis. Or if for some reason a person does not wish to go through long and costly psychoanalysis, I might consider it. I am not a physician, and I limit my work with hypnosis to research or to selected individuals whom medical doctors have been unable to help.

The First Stage

To begin the hypnosis, I ask my subject to stretch out on the celebrated psychiatrist's couch. (A person can be hypnotized while standing up or sitting down, too, but taking the weight off your feet helps you relax and thus makes the job a little easier for the hypnotist.) I generally use subdued lighting in the room, in back of the subject so that concentrated light cannot disturb his or her drifting off into sleep. The room is neither too cold nor too warm, and extraneous noises are shut out as much as possible. As I work in a city, some noises will continue to intrude, but I take care of this problem through suggestion early in the hypnosis; I tell the subject not to pay attention to any noises or sounds other than my voice. This usually works.

Once the subject is comfortable, I ask him or her to imagine being in a movie theater watching a Western. Next, the picture ends, the last horses gallop off the screen, and my subject is left watching an empty silver screen for a moment or two. Then I suggest that the subject feels tired and should take a little nap. I imply that it is perfectly all right to sleep now, since the subject is quite alone—I don't count—and he or she need not have any reservations about taking a brief rest. I tell my subject that various parts of his or her body are feeling a little heavy now—first the arms, one by one, and then the legs, and now the whole body. The person feels this, I assure you.

I next tell my subject that he or she will go to sleep when I have counted to ten, and will stay asleep until I give the command to awaken. I start to count slowly, with a decided rhythmic cadence, which is very important. Nothing puts a person to sleep faster than monotony of a kind—witness the effect of the movement and noise of a train in motion, with its recurrent noise patterns and bumps, or the loud ticking of a clock, or the effect of a rocking cradle on a baby. While I count, I intermingle such reassuring words as "peaceful," "quiet," "safe," "secure."

Not every subject is asleep at the count of ten. Many require a repeat pattern, either because they have not yet become used to me or because their threshold of consciousness is unusually high. Some people simply do not let go easily, and it can require great patience and skill to pry them loose from their clinging consciousnesses. Also, a first hypnosis takes far more effort and time than subsequent sessions because the subject and hypnotist must get to know each other a little. Mutual confidence and a close relationship are essential for good results. So I repeat the process, and at the same time indicate that we are going to go down some steps together. The subject will not hear or see anything at all except my voice. I then command "one-step. . . two-step. . . deeper, deeper down. . . three-step. . . four-step. . . deep. . . deep. . . five-step. . ." and so forth until we reach ten, which I boom out rather strongly. I may even repeat the word "ten," as this is the key sound suggested as the point of sleep earlier. Now the good subject should at least be beginning to drift off.

Next I say that we must now go down to the sea, further away from the world. Again, the subject will be quite alone there, enjoying the sea and the clear blue sky and the pleasant, mild wind—all symbols of contentment and security. Then I count again, slowly, in the same rhythmic pattern as before: "One-step. . . two-step. . . three-step. . . down, further down. . . you are going down some more steps. . . four-step. . . five step. . . ," and so on.

The Second Stage

When we finally we reach the tenth step, we have achieved what is called the second stage in hypnosis. A proper subject is now asleep, but will respond to my voice commands without awakening.

Some hypnotists, especially the stage kind, now make the subject perform physical tests to prove that he or she is indeed "under." For instance, they may poke a hypnotized subject with a needle to prove that he or she does not feel the pain. There is also the stiff-as-a-board test, in which the subject is made stiff, in what is called a cataleptic condition, and may be made to lie across two chair backs without collapsing. I deplore such tactics. Except as part of a specific scientific experiment, such tests are unnecessary and sometimes dangerous. You can get the same results with verbal exploration.

In the second stage of hypnosis, it is important that nothing disturb the subject and bring him or her out unexpectedly. I therefore usually continue right on to the final, third stage—that is, deep hypnosis—if, in my judgment, the subject is capable of it at this time.

The Third Stage

The procedure for going from the second to the third stage of hypnosis is essentially the same as before. But now I suggest, in a low, measured voice, that the subject must continue to sleep—in fact, cannot possibly awaken unless and until I so order. However, the subject may answer any question I put to him or her without either awakening or opening his or her eyes.

After a moment, I begin to question the patient by asking what his or her name is. If for any reason hypnosis has not "taken," or has not fully taken, the question will recall the subject to the normal, conscious condition. Usually he or she will say, "Oh, but I'm not asleep," or "I'm not out yet," or something to that effect. What to do then? Start all over again. Patience is a virtue, especially when you hypnotize someone. There are no shortcuts. However, a good hypnotic subject should be really under now. Once under, he or she stays under. Now I can safely question the subject, from time to time reminding him or her not to awaken until I say to do so. This may be necessary especially when I ask a question that involves an emotional reaction.

After I establish the subject's name and age, I proceed in one of two directions, depending on the purpose of the hypnosis—whether the subject is seeking help with some type of problem, or we are engaged in psychic research. If my subject needs hypnotherapy to cut out cigarettes, for instance, I will suggest that he or she will feel extreme reluctance whenever the urge to smoke strikes, and will immediately drop the idea. Or I may tell the subject to substitute some harmless move, like taking a sip of water, instead. If the subject has come to me for some unresolved problem that is psychological or social rather than medical, I question him or her about the problem, and the person's subconscious mind will speak to me. In thus unwrapping the person's ego and allowing the true self to speak freely, I also draw repressed emotions out of hiding and into the tape recorder. I can then make certain suggestions to improve the person's habits or thinking patterns. If a feeling of inferiority is the problem, I may suggest and implant a more positive, self-confident attitude toward life. If hostility comes to the fore, I may suggest more tolerance. Each case is different. A good hypnotist does not indulge in experimentation, but merely helps the subject strengthen inherent but unused moral values.

If the hypnosis has been undertaken for purposes of psychic research, I may ask the subject to project him- or herself into a certain place and describe what he or she sees. This is controlled astral projection or traveling clairvoyance. Or I may attempt to do regression, first suggesting that the subject is five years younger. Then I ask the subject his or her age, and ask for descriptions of home, family, and friends. I repeat this procedure a few more times. When I arrive at the age-two level of regression, I suggest that the subject now take another step, beyond birth. This is the most exciting part of the whole procedure. I ask the subject to be minus two, then minus five years, and so forth. At each level I ask for description of conditions, name, and so on.

When the purpose of the hypnosis has been achieved, I instruct the subject to return to full consciousness. If he or she seems to have any hesitation about waking up, I may have to return once again to the first stage, and then immediately bring the subject up again to full consciousness. Most people who undergo hypnosis feel very refreshed and rested afterwards, without stress or any of the symptoms that might have been present prior to the hynotherapy. In some cases, I program the subject not to remember anything that was done under hypnosis, especially if it involves traumatic past-life material. After all, I have the information on tape. Depending on the subject, however, and how deeply he or she went "under," the effectiveness of my commands, including the command to forget, will be 100 percent or less. In some cases, a subject remembers everything despite my command to forget, especially if he or she was anxious about hypnosis to begin with. It is imperative, therefore, that a professional hypnotherapist suggest a feeling of general well-being as a result of the session, in addition to whatever other suggestions are given.

Hypnosis is 90 percent subject and 10 percent hypnotist. But it is that 10 percent that unlocks the 90 percent, which is why a positive rapport between subject and hypnotist is so important. If there is a good rapport between the two, hypnosis usually works, and can be beneficial both medically and psychologically, as well as for psychic research.

8

PAST LIVES, REINCARNATION MEMORIES, AND THE PSYCHIC

Reincarnation is the return of the true self (or soul) after death to earthly existence in another life. Belief in reincarnation is common throughout the world, particularly in Asian cultures. In the Far East, reincarnation is widely accepted as a matter of fact because many Eastern religions have incorporated this concept into their belief systems. In Tibet, the idea of reincarnation has also been a practical way of government. A high lama, it is believed, is always reincarnated in a child, and it is the often difficult job of the priests to locate the child into which the lama has chosen to reincarnate. Guided by delicate signs, and perhaps by the deceased lama himself (though that is problematic because it would suggest he is not reincarnated after all), they find the young successor and then groom him for priesthood.

Less well known are passages in the Bible that hint at the idea of reincarnation in Jewish culture. In one passage, Jesus' disciples tell him that some people believe him to be the reincarnation of the prophet Elijah. This is an extension of a tradition that appears earlier, in the Hebrew Scriptures —that Elijah himself was Moses come back to earth.

In some African societies, the reincarnated spirits of the ancestors are looked to for guidance and also play major roles in government. This concept can be found as well in the native Haitian religion called voodoo—which, by the way, is nothing like the popular conception (or, rather, misconception) of it.

THE NATURE OF REINCARNATION MEMORIES

The concept of karma holds that the object of existence is to achieve a certain level of perfection and that the soul makes a fresh start from incarnation to incarnation (lifetime to lifetime) until this is achieved; at this point, no further return to a bodily existence is necessary. During each incarnation, we undergo certain experiences and face certain tests that determine whether we will advance up the ladder of spiritual development or head downward toward a more earthbound existence. This, in a nutshell, is the basic structure of the Eastern belief in reincarnation. It has never been proved scientifically, of course—but, by the same token, no one can prove it is false, either.

According to the classic idea of reincarnation, memories of one lifetime are supposed to be wiped out completely prior to the beginning of the next journey in the body. However, there seem to be a limited number of cases in which the system simply doesn't work as it should, and the result is a phenomenon called the reincarnation memory. Nature is basically perfect, but deviations from the norm do crop up. While we all come back to other lives, those whose past lives were somehow irregular seem to get a sort of "bonus" in the form of memory; they may be able to recall snatches of their past lives, whether directly, through recurrent dreams, or through hypnotic regression.

It appears that we all reincarnate, but the length of the periods between lives and the frequency of return may vary. One popular notion concerning reincarnation is that people reincarnate together in groups, sometimes changing social positions in the process for the purpose of learning certain spiritual values. However, the evidence for group reincarnation does not seem to be strong, and it certainly is not as scientifically sound as the material on the basic validity of reincarnation itself. Similarly, I have seen no credible evidence whatever of transmigration—that people now living as humans may have lived before in other forms, chiefly as animals—which is part of certain East Indian belief systems.

Memories From Other Lives

Some people have startlingly clear and detailed memories of circumstances and experiences that could not have come from their own lives, and that make sense only if looked at as residue from past lives. Others have vague memories of previous existences that are not as clear-cut as they would like. This is not surprising, since, if the philosophies of the East are correct, we are not *supposed* to have a clear memory—or any memory at all—of past lives.

One interesting thing that I have learned from both my own experience and from the many cases I have investigated over the years is that reincarnation memories usually occur in people who possess no psychic inclinations whatever, either prior to realizing the reincarnation memory or afterwards. There are exceptions—it is possible for a psychic person, whether an amateur or a professional medium, to have reincarnation memories separate from his or her psychic gift— but this is quite rare. The majority of reincarnation-memory cases that I have verified involve people who have no known psychic abilities and no interest in the subject. In addition, detailed and specific reincarnation material appears to surface only if the prior life was terminated violently or otherwise cut short or unfulfilled in some manner.

Two truly astonishing cases were reported by an Indian researcher, H.N. Banerjee.

> A young boy claimed to be the reincarnation of a man from another village who had died of a fever some years before the boy was born. His parents agreed to test the claim by bringing him to the dead man's family. The widow asked the boy to tell her of some specific event in their life. He replied by describing in detail a certain violent quarrel they had had, and also told the astonished widow intimate details about their conjugal life that no one else could have known. Without difficulty or hesitation, he found the house the couple had lived in and recognized local people and conditions, although he had never been there or met them before. He walked around the house and farm, recalling incidents and things he remembered

vividly, and he took all the curious people to the attic (an unusual feature there). He told them that that had been his room—that he had taken his wife there the day they were married, and he had died there, at the age of twenty-one. He then asked the widow, "Where is the sari I brought you from Agra?" The woman was startled. No one else had known about this gift.

As soon as she could talk, a young child began insisting that she was a cleaning woman and had to be about her job. She gave a name, and eventually the case was investigated and traced back to Spain, where the identity of a woman by that name was indeed established. It turned out that the child had been born at almost the exact moment that the cleaning woman had died. What is more, the child never became normal in the ordinary sense, but continued the life and memories of her former existence.

Cases of recognition and verification by no means happen only in India, traditionally a country friendly to the idea of karma and rebirth. They have happened in England, where a child vividly recalled freezing to death with her father in a hut in the country. The facts of the case in question bore this out, yet the child could not have known them.

Reincarnation memories happen elsewhere, too. The cases I have investigated are all from the West, which disproves the popularly held belief that reincarnation is something only people in the East accept as true.

Pamela Wollenberg, a young girl from northern Illinois, had recurrent dreams about Scotland in the year 1600. Prominent in her dreams were two names she did not understand at all, Ruthven and Gowrrie, and the words "I leapt." I investigated the case for many months, using hypnotic regression and doing local research in Scotland. Eventually, this led to detailed information about two names in the Scotland of 1600 of whom Pamela could not possibly have known, the Ruthvens and the Gowrries, who actually belonged to the same extended family. In 1600, two Gowrrie brothers were involved in a conspiracy to kidnap the young King James VI. One of the ladies Gowrrie had "leapt" from one tower of the castle to another to escape her mother's pursuit when a young man had shared her chamber that night. None of this material was easily found by me, and none of it would have been accessible to Pamela.

A woman from a small town in rural Pennsylvania visited a town near Atlanta, Georgia, and experienced sudden reincarnation memories when she passed a house, now in disrepair, that had figured prominently in an earlier life of hers during the Civil War period. Months of work followed, during which I regressed her several times, visited her Pennsylvania hometown in this life, and researched the rich material that came from her while under regressive hypnosis and in dreams. It concerned a previous life and death, all of which I was able to check out.

Of course, the question arises whether we can always separate legitimate evidence for reincarnation from, say, a person's psychic ability. It is possible, for instance, that knowledge that seems to be reincarnation memory comes not from the person's own former life memory, but from another person whose communication from the other side is the true source of that knowledge. Another possible explanation is that a discarnate entity (a soul without current bodily existence) may be using a living person to express unfulfilled desires. However, if this were to be a fitting explanation, the person would certainly show evidence of a deep trance. But in all the reports I have of credible reincarnation cases, the person has been fully awake and quite normal—except for the insistence that he or she is someone else.

Déjà Vu

Much larger in number than the number of cases of verifiable reincarnation memory are cases of the phenomenon classified as the *déjà vu* experience by orthodox psychiatry. This is the uncanny feeling of having been somewhere before, or, on meeting a stranger for the first time, getting the impression that you have met him or her before—somewhere, sometime, but you do not know where or when.

There is hardly a person alive who has not had this sensation at one time or another, if only in a vague sort of way. The conventional psychiatric explanation for this is that, for some reason, we occasionally open the wrong memory door in our consciousness—instead of pressing the button marked "never saw him before," we press the one marked "I've met him before." But psychiatry does not tell us why we do this, or how.

Since the reaction is practically instantaneous, I would venture to say that it is not up to us to press anything at all. Rather, the radiation, or what have you, emanating from the stranger instantly brings back something from our unconscious past. If this is so, it may well be that we are dealing with reincarnation memories, but that we cannot recall these vestigial memories beyond an automatic reaction when something or someone out of a past life pops up in our present one. That's about all the Universal Law normally allows us to know about past lives. Thus, while we have all led other lives, information about them is not normally accessible to us and we must probe deeply if we are to find it.

There are also numerous cases on record of a type of *déjà vu* in which a person sees and hears a scene take place in his or her conscious life and knows, at that instant, that he or she has seen and heard this before. Some parapsychologists offer an alternate explanation to reincarnation in such cases. They would say that the person has had a precognitive experience, either in the dream state or in the waking state, but that it took place so quickly that the person forgot the impression. When the scene takes place in reality, the person remembers having seen it sometime before, and "it all comes back to him." In most such cases, we cannot prove that the individuals involved had such psychic impressions, premonitions, or other precognitive experiences, because they never write them down or report them to competent witnesses. And quite naturally so, since they did not pay attention to them (or even notice them) at the time they occurred—if they occurred.

This explanation for *déjà vu* may be valid in some cases, but certainly not in all. Take, for instance, the case of an American soldier during World War II:

An American G.I. stationed in Europe was sent as part of the advance guard in a military detachment entering a village in Belgium. They were looking for enemy stragglers. But as he and two other soldiers rounded a street corner, the G.I. in question made straight for a certain house. "My house, my house!" he cried out, to the puzzlement of the other two. They entered the now-empty house and started up the stairs to the second floor. The other two men started to question their comrade about his claim that this was "his house." Very agitated by now, he assured them it was, and that he had grown up there "a long time ago." To prove his point, he told the others what they would see when they entered the upper story; he described a painting that would be found there, and all the furnishings in the room they had not yet entered. Sure enough, when they got there, everything was exactly as he had said.

Was this man merely walking down a false memory lane? Was he remembering a precognitive experience? On the whole, I find the explanation of a reincarnation memory more likely, and, even though we have not yet fully understood how the system works, there is a system to all this, and one day we may better understand it.

Barry Bingham, the newspaper editor, had had a recurrent dream over a period of several months. In it, he found himself approaching a very tall and beautiful building that stood in an open green space. The scene was always bathed in the serene light of a morning that follows a rainy night. Some time later, while in England, Bingham went to see Salisbury Cathedral. He had never been there before, and as he approached it, he suddenly stood stock still, hardly daring to breathe. This ancient church, in its setting of dewy greensward, was the building of his dream in every detail. He knew every feature of its architecture, and felt as though he had spent years in that very spot. Stumbling into the church, still dazed and awed, he moved up the aisle and sat down for a moment to rest. As he raised his eyes, he saw directly before him a memorial to a bishop whose name, he realized, was that of a remote ancestor of his. The man had been the bishop there for seventeen years. In that moment, Bingham realized that it was his ancestor who had passed across that very spot of ground, over and over again each day, for years. He was the man who knew that scene, as well as he knew the palm of his own hand. But the bishop had died in 1246, and had been laid to his rest seven long centuries ago.

This case is particularly interesting as it offers two possible avenues of explanation. Since an ancestor of the subject is involved, it could be a matter of psychic communication. Or perhaps Barry Bingham actually was a living person at the time of the event he experienced—possibly even his own ancestor. Scientifically speaking, however, we can state only that, whatever the explanation, he had an extraordinary psychic experience.

I myself went to Salisbury, at his request, because of this experience, and also because someone else had managed to photograph what appeared to be a ghostly manifestation in the old church. I have no emotional ties to Salisbury, and I felt nothing unusual. But I have been to the Scottish Highlands and felt terribly sure I have lived there before. No facts, just a feeling.

So it goes with *déjà vu* sometimes. You cannot always pin it down, but to dismiss it lightly is like closing the door on one of the most intriguing facets of human experience. I often hear from people with "having-been-there-before" experiences, and I am always eager to follow up on them, so that some day we may link the living with their former incarnations so convincingly that skeptical orthodox science will accept the evidence as true.

DEMONSTRATING THE VALIDITY OF REINCARNATION MEMORIES

There are basically two different approaches to reincarnation-memory research today. One is the painstaking and very difficult approach that involves the objective verification of such memories. To my mind, this is the only valid approach if it is proof we want, not just wishful thinking.

The other approach—which is, unfortunately, far more

popular—is the "past-life reading" that certain mediums will do for anyone willing to pay the price. For the most part, these amount to uncritical wallowing in fanciful worlds that may or may not have existed—certainly neither I nor anyone else can no more prove that they *didn't* than the believers can prove that they did or do (*see* The Truth About Channeling, page 108). The only past-life readings I respect as perhaps having some basis in fact are those undertaken by the late Edgar Cayce, a psychic healer and one of the most renowned mediums in history. The reason I feel this way about his life readings, all recorded at the Virginia Beach headquarters of the Association for Research and Enlightenment, is that other aspects of Cayce's mediumship have been proved to be accurate and truly outstanding; so on the basis of his other achievements, I respect these readings as worthy of study.

Nevertheless, there are readers who will tell you that you were so-and-so in ancient Egypt or some other fanciful locale. Very rarely were you a common, ordinary person. On the contrary, you probably consorted with Cleopatra herself, or with other well-known historical figures. And the reason you are attracted to your present mate is that you were married once before some centuries ago.

Now, the strange thing is that, for all we know, any or all of this may be perfectly true. However, it is impossible to verify one way or the other, and for that very reason, it is worthless for the purposes of scientific research. In some cases, some of the material may even be verifiable, if the proper safeguards are used. If the reader has no access to the type of information he or she supplies, and names, events, and other material supplied are checked out later and found to be correct, you would at least have some corroboration that such people and events actually existed. But you still would lack proof of any kind of link between them and the subject of the life reading. I am not attacking the idea of tracing back evidence for reincarnation. In fact, I am in favor of a concerted effort in this direction. But I am against unproven or unprovable information being sold to gullible people. Only when something truly definitive turns up that

The Truth About Channeling

The popularity of certain paranormal practices and beliefs seems to run in cycles. After World War I, bereaved friends and family members frequented spiritualist séances in droves, in the hope their lost loved ones would talk with them from the Great Beyond. A more recent fad is channeling, a practice in which, supposedly, the spirit of an individual no longer living speaks through the body of a living person. Many of these so-called entities are claimed by their promoters to be mysterious persons who lived many thousands of years ago. Others are represented as famous historical figures of one type or another.

On the surface, channelers look and act like trance mediums. They close their eyes, or roll them dramatically, before going into an altered state. Then a voice claiming to be that of someone other than the channeler speaks to the audience or client. However, unlike trance mediums, channelers tend to respond to questions concerning the personal background or real names of their "entities" with platitudes about the high level of their mission, or fantasy names and circumstances that cannot be verified—or, in some cases, material that sounds as if it might be capable of scientific verification, but that turns out later to be impossible to trace in any known records.

Furthermore, even if we assume that there really may be entities—real persons long deceased—speaking through most of these channelers, would it not be reasonable to expect the personalities we are hearing from to enlighten us with definite, specific, and truly detailed knowledge of their times and places? Or assume for the moment that some very illustrious historical figure chose to manifest through a channeler. Would it not be likely that the personality, character, and style of the person would somehow come through, even if English was not that individual's native language? Unfortunately, the "entities" that come through most channelers fall sadly short on these tests as well.

I once encountered a young woman who makes a living as a psychic who said that she was the channel for St. Thomas Aquinas, the thirteenth-century theologian and philosopher. And what did St. Thomas have to say to us mortals today? A few general platitudes about the world needing to save itself. No deep thoughts about theology, history, or philosophy. This St. Thomas was strictly unreal. But the woman insisted, "I channel his essence." Essence? Impersonating a saint?

What makes the average channeler run is twofold: On the one hand, an eager audience of followers to feed the ego (and often also to supply money); on the other hand, the opportunity for otherwise ordinary individuals to act out fantasies satisfying neglected cravings within their personalities. Channeling has become big business, including not only in-person seminars where the faithful gather and (at a stiff price) are allowed to partake of the "pearls of wisdom" dropping from the lips of their channelers, but also audiotapes, books, magazines, follow-up books, more seminars, and question-and-answer sessions at which people seek the counsel of the channeling "entity" in solving their personal problems. Indeed, eager followers believe that the pronouncements of these supposed personalities can be interpreted to present a new, world-shaking understanding of and approach to life. In general, however, nothing could be further from the truth. Any fairly intelligent person with a smattering of knowledge of psychology and religion could come up with advice similar to that of your average channeler. You certainly don't need the wisdom of the ages to do it!

Anyone with a gift for turning a clever phrase can claim to be channeling some exotic long-ago personality or "master." Some psychic researchers, while acknowledging the sad lack of evidence for most channeling "entities," suggest that the process of dealing with channeled material may nevertheless help us to know ourselves better. Perhaps it does. And nothing in the world is an absolute. No doubt not every "ascended master" is a figment of the imagination. But some kind of evidence should be required before any type of communication is accepted as genuine.

In the end, the proof of the pudding is in the eating. If you want sugar-coated platitudes or a mystical "adventure," your average channeler will probably do nicely. If you are truly interested in communicating with an entity of higher intelligence or certain specific knowledge, however, you ought to be more demanding with respect to the quality of evidence in such communications. Always remember that proof lies in how specific and verifiable the material or message obtained is. If only generalities are obtained, beware.

is not readily accessible to the medium and is independently corroborated do we have a genuine case for reincarnation.

The number of cases of reincarnation memories is not as large as, say, the number of plausible ghost cases—by "plausible," I mean a recent event, observed by competent witnesses, and properly researched by people qualified to do so. Reincarnation material also is not as spectacular, and consequently does not command as much attention, as the appearance of ghosts. In the end, my position on reincarnation memories is the same as it is regarding so-called unidentified flying objects (UFOs): If 90 percent of all reported incidents can be explained by ordinary means and 10 percent cannot, then that is 10 percent too many for comfort. Thus, even if only a handful of solidly substantiated cases of reincarnation memory exist, and cannot be explained in any other way, then we have a scientific case for the existence of this phenomenon.

EXPLORING PAST LIVES

Once, when I was taping a pilot for a proposed television program in Cleveland, a group practicing "suggestive regression" under the control and guidance of a New Age group leader caught my attention and I proceeded to watch a session. Each of the dozen or so participants—all of them women, by the way—went into a meditative state first, presumably to tap their deeper levels of consciousness, including past-life memories. Each in turn then spoke up and told me who they had been before. At least two of the ladies were sure they had been Egyptians, but it was the young housewife who assured me that she had been both Isadora Duncan, the dancer, and the Queen of Sheba, King Solomon's lover, who particularly interested me. I soon realized that this was all a harmless fantasy (besides, I myself knew of at least two other Isadora Duncans in other cities), so I did not even attempt a serious investigation.

Some people blame "past lives" for things they do in this life that would otherwise be frowned upon. For instance, a publisher of some renown divorced his wife when he met a young woman he fancied immediately. His reason: They had been together in another lifetime, and needed to resume in this one!

Anybody who wishes to believe he or she lived before as someone markedly different (and probably more interesting) is, of course, welcome to the fantasy. But I feel less charitable toward the increasing number of casual practitioners giving "past-life readings" at a price. As far as I know, none of these individuals uses professional hypnotic regression to see whether there is, in fact, any memory of a possible previous incarnation. Instead, they prefer to do their readings intuitively and generally, in terms that are incapable of true verification in books or records of any kind.

One particularly crass case I know of involved a woman who had been complaining of pains in her wrists and feet. She had not been able to get a medical explanation that satisfied her (such as arthritis or rheumatism or just tension), but she met a "past-life reader" who had the right answer, apparently: Those pains were due to crucifixion at the time of Jesus! With that, the pains seemed to cease, or at least she had an explanation that hastened her cure.

In another case, a psychiatrist who includes reincarnation trauma work in his treatment of patients, using a trance medium as his assistant, told a patient that the terrible pains in his legs were a consequence of his having lost his legs in another lifetime. The patient accepted the explanation, and learned to live with his problem. But unless there are specific data, such as names, dates, and places given, this type of "past-life" material is rarely more than just another psychological trick— even if it turns out to be beneficial to the patient.

What, then, is one to do to avoid being taken in by "past-life readers"—who, incidentally, may well believe fully in their work and its authenticity? There are not that many conscious frauds among them, but there are quite a few self-deluded people—and even they, on occasion, help some clients by making them feel important or interesting. If an honest quest for truth is what you are looking for, certain precautions are in order regarding dealing with such practitioners.

To begin with, never talk about yourself or who you think you might have been in a prior life. Do not answer questions posed by the reader along these lines, either. If the reader tells you of an existence in another life, insist on details; when, where, what name. Chances are, the reader will do one of two things: make them up to sound substantial, or tell you, "Sorry, I don't get those details." Either way, take everything you are told with a big grain of salt.

True, acceptable past life evidence is always possible. But in all the years of my practice in parapsychology, I have found that such material is almost never obtained by searching deliberately in the hope of "finding something." Instead, signs suggesting that you may have a memory of a past life are more likely to surface on their own. Such signs include recurrent dreams, especially identical dreams that keep coming back and are well recalled on awakening; extended *déjà vu* experiences that occur in a place you have not been before and that contain particulars regarding the previous connection; and, finally, knowledge or ability in a field not acquired consciously in this lifetime, such as the ability to speak a strange foreign language, or technical knowledge, or "memories" of places and situations that you are not familiar with in normal life, and that you have had no access to through books, newspapers, television, or other ordinary sources.

If such signs are present, regressive hypnosis (see Chapter 7) may be able to draw out the past-life memory. Of course, this ought to be done by a professionally trained person, not just a layperson who one day decided he or she was a "past-life reader." If you observe real signs and act on them appropriately, pursuing the quest for evidence of past lives can be stimulating and truly worthwhile.

9

PSYCHIC DREAMS

Much psychic material comes to the surface in dreams. This is because it is easier for such information to reach the mind when the mind is not otherwise occupied and is in a resting state. Unfortunately, ever since the arrival of psychoanalysis, dream material has been subjected to interpretation by the medical fraternity. Only when a dream is so strongly psychic in content, and the content becomes reality at a later date, may a psychiatrist admit—grudgingly—that there may be something to the psychic explanation.

From time immemorial, dreams have been thought to be a way in which God could manifest directly to the sleeper, bringing messages or orders that would not reach the person in the more prosaic daylight hours. The Bible is full of these incidents, from the stories of Moses and the prophets in the Hebrew Scriptures to the story of Mary and Joseph in the New Testament.

Shakespeare refers to "the stuff that dreams are made on," but never comes to grips with the nature of dreams themselves. Modern psychiatrists are sure they have the one and only explanation for dreaming—that the unconscious mind is acting up. Eastern mystics are equally sure all dreams are prophetic, and must be interpreted symbolically.

There is doubtless some truth in all of these dream theories, but none contains all of the truth. It is difficult to explain the nature of dreams satisfactorily in terms of modern scientific thought. This is because dreams are not experiences in themselves; rather, dreaming is a condition in which several different types of experiences may occur. In other words, just as the significance of the act of walking depends largely on who is doing it, where, and how, so dreaming by itself is not an absolute condition.

The term "dream" covers a multitude of situations. There are four main classifications of dreams: dreams caused by physical conditions; dreams of a prophetic nature; dreams in which the dreamer travels; and psychological dreams.

An examination of these categories reveals that the dream state is actually a greater form of awareness than is the waking state. The limitations imposed by the time-space continuum of the waking state have no meaning in the dream state, in which the physical body is temporarily excluded from participating in events. Since the experiences of the inner, etheric body take place on the thought plane, in which physical and time barriers are removed, events seem more immediate and stronger, as if they were actually happening on the physical level.

DREAMS CAUSED BY PHYSICAL CONDITIONS

Dreams caused by physical conditions include nightmares and anxiety dreams. A typical example of a person having this type of experience is the man who overeats shortly before bedtime and then has illogical nightmares. Such anxiety states are induced by malfunctioning of the biochemical system of the body, with resulting pressures that create the false dream images. Illness and high fever can have similar effects.

DREAMS OF A PROPHETIC NATURE

This category includes clairvoyant and warning dreams, prophecies, and the like. Prophetic dreams may contain both precognitive information and material suggestive of reincarnation memories.

As a young woman, Helen Ann Elsner served in the Army

medical corps at Fort Belvoir, Virginia. One night she had a dream about a young man, a fellow corpsman, in which she saw him in patient's pajamas and felt that she was the hospital aide taking care of him. She saw herself straightening the covers of his bed as part of the evening care when he reached up and tried to kiss her. At that moment, a woman Helen did not know walked into the room, and the corpsman said, "There's my ex-wife. I didn't know she knew where I was, let alone sick."

Several weeks later, when Helen came to the cafeteria, she saw the corpsman wearing hospital pajamas and immediately recalled her dream. He asked her to come to his ward. As she was standing by his bed and talking about a book she had read, the corpsman looked up and interrupted their conversation with the comment, "There's my ex-wife I didn't know she knew where I was, let alone sick."

Michael Bentine, the actor friend of mine mentioned in Chapter 3, was planning a trip to the country. A few days before the journey, he had a vivid dream in which he saw himself driving his car at great speed. Suddenly there was a sharp bend in the road, and another car's headlights appeared practically in front of him. A crash followed, a head-on collision. My friend took this warning seriously, but set out on his trip as planned. It was nighttime, and he was driving on a road where he had never been before. Suddenly there was a sharp bend in the road, and he at once recognized the stretch of road as being identical to the one in his dream. With this realization came the memory of the rest of his dream. He slowed down at once—just in time to see the oncoming headlights of another car, which would have hit him head-on if he had not been forewarned.

Kaye Schoerning, a Hillsboro, Texas, nurse, read in the local newspaper one day that three gunmen had robbed a Sears store in a town to the southwest. That night, she dreamed the same men would come the following day at exactly 12:00 midnight to rob their local Sears store. She mentioned the dream to her father, who was the mayor of the town, and asked him to do something about it. Her father shook his head. Why would three gunmen want to rob such a small store? But she insisted, and he called the police in. At exactly 12:00 midnight, the three men appeared at the store and tried to rob it. Because of the warning, however, the police captured the thieves.

A great deal of research and analysis has been done on the incidence of precognitive dreams among average people. It has been found that almost everyone dreams, but that most people do not remember their dreams. It has also been found that precognition is a fairly common ability. Tested and confirmed examples of clairvoyant dreams exist by the thousands in the files of universities and psychical research societies.

Barbara Moeller, a woman with genuine psychic talent who works as an office manager for a painting and decorating company in Omaha, Nebraska, had a dream in which she had left work and was driving along a narrow street to the main highway when her car struck a small boy. In the dream, she saw the details of the accident very clearly. The boy's boot flew off and blood streamed down his face. Upset, she told her husband and also a cousin about the dream, and made sure to be extremely careful every time she drove along the particular street in her dream. One day some weeks later, however, a young boy darted out suddenly from between a car and a truck and into the street in front of Barbara's car. She slammed on her brakes immediately, but it was too late. Her car struck the boy. Just as in the dream, he lost his boot and his nose bled profusely. Fortunately, he was not seriously injured.

When she was only eight years old, Mary Pugar had a dream in which she pulled back a curtain in the room where her mother was sleeping and the large curtain pole came down with a crash, almost killing her. She forgot about the dream until forty-two years later, when she was just about to leave for the central Oregon school where she was a teacher. Her mother, who was living with her, said she was going to go to the woodshed to get some wood. Mary put her books down and said she would go get it instead. She had just started to pull the shed door open when a slight sound made her hesitate. The next thing she knew, a two-by-four from over the door fell down in front of her. In that instant, she recalled the dream and realized that if her mother had gone for the wood, she would not have hesitated, but would have gone right in, since she was hard of hearing and would not have heard the slight sound.

That a person may experience an event long before it actually occurs is not a matter for speculation. It is a proven fact. It is also a most challenging fact, for what are we to make of our free will if the future has already been decided? I am convinced that events are stationary and it is we who travel toward them along the time track (see Chapter 4). Therefore, the fine line of demarcation between present and future is really nonexistent.

DREAMS IN WHICH THE DREAMER TRAVELS

Dreams in which you seem to travel to strange places and be among people you may or may not know, all at a physical distance from your home, may be related to astral projection. These dreams are often remembered rather clearly, and the experiences lack the confusion and illogical associations so common to ordinary dreams. In fact, this is the type of dream in which you may think you are not dreaming at all, but are really there.

In these dreams, people find themselves in distant places, and see and even talk to strangers or good friends. Many cases of this type have been even verified on the "other end"—that is, by the people visited by the dreamer in the dream state. To the people visited, the dreamer seems to be his or her usual self, only to disappear into thin air when challenged or spoken to.

> A man dreamed he was in a Turkish bath, where the attendant asked him for his papers. He replied that he had no such papers, and strongly wished to leave the unpleasant situation at once. Immediately he found himself back in his own bed. The following day, as chance would have it, a friend took him to the same Turkish bath. There stood the attendant our dreamer had argued with in his dream state. When the attendant saw him, he angrily pounced on him and again demanded his papers. Also, he wanted to know how he had so suddenly disappeared from under his very nose the night before!

What actually happens in *these* dream states (usually involuntary, but occasionally produced at will), is the following. The bond between the physical body and the astral, or etheric, body, which is the seat of the personality, is weakened. The person—that is, the person's etheric self—then wanders off, is drawn to various places and people, and, being fully conscious except for the absence of a physical body, acts and reacts as if nothing were unusual about his or her appearance. In this state, distance is of no importance, and it takes only a fraction of a second to cover thousands of miles. The dreamer has almost total control over his or her movements, since the logical mind functions properly during the projection. However, it takes great discipline to control the thoughts that can propel the personality all over the globe at the very moment of desire. When the dreamer wishes to return to bed, he or she so *thinks*, and instantly is back at home. (For a more detailed discussion of astral projection, see Chapter 6.)

PSYCHOLOGICAL DREAMS

These dreams contain symbolic expressions of the unconscious mind. To the psychoanalyst, all dreams have symbolic and analytical meanings. What exactly these symbolic meanings are has been interpreted in various ways. Sigmund Freud thought that all dream images were sexually motivated. Carl Jung and his disciples came to believe differently.

I am convinced that many dreams have such meanings, but not all of them do. Signs of the true psychological dream include the dreamer doing things he or she cannot do in real life; solving problems he or she cannot solve when awake; or experiencing conditions and situations he or she secretly desires but has been unable to experience, whether because of worldly restrictions, mental or emotional blocks, or some combination of these. In this type of dream, the dreamer is the main character, and everything else revolves around that individual. In the other types of dreams, we are more of observers or visitors.

Certainly we must not allow ourselves to slip into the superstition of ancient times, when each and every dream was believed to hold some prophetic meaning. Yet it is clear that two out of the four types of dreams people experience are not properly a subject for the psychiatrist, but belong to the realm of parapsychology. Precognition (and, in some cases, memories from other lifetimes) constitute the explanation for one group, and out-of-body experiences for the other. What these two types of dreams do *not* present is any connection with psychological symbolism, suppressed feelings, or unresolved trauma.

Dreaming is not an adjunct to sleep, or something that happens from time to time. It happens *all the time*, but we are not always able to remember or to be aware of our dreams. Indeed, throughout our lives we are either awake or "adream," an active state that is a kind of natural setting for psychic experiences and the emergence of psychic material.

10

THE GIFT
OF PSYCHIC HEALING

Psychic ability can take many forms. One of the most valuable is the gift of psychic healing, which can occur in anyone who is psychic, either in combination with other psychic talents or alone.

Psychic healing is as old as humankind itself. It is the treatment of ailments, both physical and mental, by the powers of the spirit—or, at any rate, by forces not yet recognized as physical in the ordinary sense. Much of the early psychic healing was done by priests or lay priests, who thought it necessary to surround their healing practices with a certain mystery in order to strengthen their patients' belief in them, and thus strengthen their will to get well. To this day, it makes a great deal of difference whether a sick person trusts his or her doctor or not. Faith cannot move mountains, perhaps, but it can surely rally the body's defense mechanisms.

THE NATURE OF PSYCHIC HEALING

In psychic healing, no medicines of any kind are used, and it is not necessary that the patient be a believer for the cure to work. Certainly faith helps—and also strengthens resistance to disease—but true psychic healing, which is often instantaneous or very nearly so, does not require such a state of mind on the part of the one undergoing it. Rather, its success depends on the healer's ability to draw enough of his or her life force into his or her hands to effect the healing.

Spiritualism, a religion that incorporates a belief in communication between living persons and the spirit world with elements of Christian belief, calls this practice spiritual healing. According to spiritualist belief, God works through the hands of the healer as the healer touches the body of the patient. However, I have found that some nonspiritualists and even some atheists have had remarkable results in healing through psychic means. Whereas a spiritualist who works as a healer will credit the help of spirit guides or spirits (who may have been doctors while in the physical world), psychic healers usually understand that the healing comes from the application of their body energies, of which they possess unusually large amounts.

Psychic healing utilizes the force present in the healer's body to destroy disease in another person's aura (the magnetic field extending somewhat beyond the physical body). The healer draws energy from his or her physical body, mainly from the two solar plexus in the back of the stomach and at the top of the head, where networks of nerve cells come together. This energy is then channelled through the healer's hands and applied to the aura of the patient. A good healer notices the discoloration of the aura that indicates illness. By placing his or her energy into the troubled areas of the aura, the healer displaces or "burns out" the diseased parts and momentarily creates a vacuum within the aura. Healthy electrically charged particles—that is, healthy energy—rush to fill these gaps. When the inner body is restored to perfect health, the parallel outer body cannot help but fall in line. The aura (or etheric body, or electromagnetic field within us) duplicates the outer, physical body in every respect except one: It extends beyond the skin slightly, usually about a quarter of an inch. Thus, a psychic healer will not touch the skin, but pass his or her hands slightly above it, because that is where the sensitive "skin" of the etheric body is. Disease clears up almost at once, or as fast as the cells can keep pace with the orders from the etheric body within.

Dean Kraft, a musician living in Brooklyn, New York, was driving home from work when he heard a strange clicking sound
and found his car doors locked, although he had not touched
the appropriate buttons. He asked, more as a joke than seriously, if there were spirits present, and to his amazement received
a response in a sort of code of clicks. At the time, he was working in a music shop, and, together with his boss, he perfected
this code until he could actually communicate with "them."

One day, he heard the horrible sounds of an automobile
crash outside the shop. He rushed to the street and found a
woman on the pavement who had been badly hurt. Something
told him to hold her in his hands until an ambulance came to
take her to the hospital. Later, when he drove home, the
unseen communicators told him, via the click code, "Tonight
your hands were used for *healing*." The musician did not
understand the message. He called the hospital to check on the
woman's condition, and was told that she was on the critical
list and would undergo surgery in the morning. But when he
called again the next day, to find out how she was doing after
the surgery, he was shocked to hear that she had been dis-
charged. Somehow, he was told, her injuries had "healed
themselves during the early hours of the morning."

Mrs. C. consulted a psychic healer in a state of abject fear; her
doctor had told her she had a growth in her throat, and surgery
was necessary. The day before surgery was scheduled, she saw
the healer. She reported experiencing a wonderful feeling of
cleansing and extreme heat coming from the hands of the healer during the treatment. When she went to the doctor afterwards, he found that the growth had completely disappeared.

Psychic healers tend to be people who have great magnet-
ism or power of personality—people whose life force seems
so strong that they can spare some of it to heal less fortunate
human beings. A psychic healer can be either a man or a
woman, or even a child, for the gift plays no favorites. If the
patient responds to psychic healing, he or she usually reports
a hot sensation in the affected part of the body, far beyond the
normal bodily warmth emanating from a hand passing an
inch away.

The use of psychic healing circles, in which several people

surround the patient, holding hands or not, is a practice in which healing energy is drawn from more than one person. If simultaneous prayer (or chanting) is involved, this can add to the available power—not necessarily because of divine intervention, but because sound in unison is a power source, and when it is directed toward the patient, it can add to the benefits of the healing attempt. In addition, some trance mediums can draw on the energies of a spirit guide and thus temporarily become healers (the subject of trance mediums will be discussed in detail in Chapter 11).

It is possible for a person who is otherwise not in the least interested in ESP or psychic phenomena to have the gift of psychic healing without realizing it, until other people say they have experienced.strange sensations when the talented one's hands were put on them or passed above them. Just like other forms of the extra sense, the power to heal can be increased through use. Once recognized, the gift should be used often.

Psychic healers have had proven successes with all types of ailments, from backaches to broken bones—even such serious afflictions as cancer, heart disease, and multiple sclerosis. Conventional physicians like to dismiss such cures as "unexpected remissions." But many of the diseases that have been helped by psychic healers are simply not the kinds of problems that disappear by themselves. The only logical conclusion, therefore, is that psychic healing can indeed result in physical changes in the body.

PSYCHIC HEALING VERSUS CONVENTIONAL MEDICINE

The basic difference between conventional medicine and the various forms of psychic healing is that psychic healing looks at the individual as a spiritual being that manifests itself through the mind as a material being. The spirit creates, and the physical body is the result. If one of the forces within the body becomes unbalanced with the others, illness results. Conventional medicine, on the other hand, thinks in terms of physical structures; you have liver disease, or lung disease, or whatever.

If we are to understand psychic healing at all, we first have to accept the duality of human nature, which forms the rational basis for the practice. That is, all people have a physical body on the outside, and a finer, inner or etheric, body underneath. It is the inner body that is the real *persona*—the soul, if you wish. Psychic healing is always holistic; the entire person—both physical body and etheric body—is healed. Indeed, one aspect cannot be treated without the other.

There are many cases on record in which psychic healing succeeded in helping where conventional medicine could not. And because it involves no drugs or invasive procedures, psychic healing is quite safe and has no side effects at all. Its use should therefore be encouraged—as long as it is used in balance with conventional medical diagnosis and care. Indeed, it is the earmark of the reliable psychic healer to have all potential patients get a regular medical checkup *first*.

HEALING PRACTICES RELATED TO PSYCHIC HEALING

In addition to psychic healing proper, there are a number of healing processes that differ from currently accepted conventional medical practice and that, in one way or another, utilize elements of the psychic. They are as old as humanity itself, and have existed in various forms and under various names since time immemorial. In ancient times, such healings were considered miraculous (or sometimes diabolic). Only in recent years has an orderly, reasonable scientific approach to studying such practices been possible. Today, more and more members of the medical profession are taking another look at these seemingly "impossible" cures.

Physical Healing

This type of unorthodox treatment, also known as "laying on of hands," has been adopted by many Christian churches (some literally, some only symbolically) as a method of healing. In this practice, the healer touches the afflicted area of the body with his or her hands, so that the healer's hands are actually slightly inside the etheric body. Although the prime force in this kind of treatment is still the psychic energy of the healer, a positive attitude toward the treatment on the part of the patient is helpful. If the healer is a priest or minister, religious faith also enters the process to some extent. Results vary, but they can be quite good in some cases.

Hypnotherapy

Hypnotherapy is a method in which the patient undergoes deep hypnosis so that he or she may effect self-healing. While the patient is under hypnosis, the healer explores emotional conflicts within the patient, removes them, and replaces them with positive, helpful suggestions. The placement of low-key commands into the patient's unconscious mind by hypnotic suggestion helps the patient to overcome his or her ailments, using his or her own psychic energies in the process. (For more information about hypnosis, see Chapter 7.)

Faith Healing

Faith healing is often confused with psychic healing, but the two are not the same. In faith healing, everything depends on three elements. First, the afflicted person must have a religious belief in the possibility of healing through divine intervention. The stronger the individual's belief, the better. Second, the patient must have unlimited confidence in the healer from whom he or she expects "the miracle." Third, a large audience—the larger the better—is usually required for the faith healing to succeed.

Successful faith healings are not necessarily the result of religious belief alone. In invoking spiritual guidance, the faith healer, first of all, unleashes within himself or herself psychic forces that are utilized to heal the sick. The expectant state of the usually desperate patient in turn spurs his or her own powers of self-healing. The result may be spontaneous cure. The reservoir of psychic energy represented by the large audience is also drawn upon to supply additional power for the process.

Occasionally, faith healing can work without an audience.

> Cecile Diamond, a fourteen-year-old girl suffering from inflammation of the brain, was given a 1-in-100 chance of survival. A spiritual healer placed an amulet in Cecile's hand and prayed. The next day, the girl felt better, and she was able to leave the hospital soon after, completely cured.

Psychic healing is based on the passing of energy from one person to another, with the healer being active and the patient being more or less passive. In faith healing, on the other hand, the patient does most of the work. The healer's role is that of catalyst; he or she uses religion (usually of a fundamentalist stripe) to suggest to the patient that God will provide healing because of the healer's fervent prayers. Many so-called faith healers, unfortunately, are charlatans or worse. They may speak of their "ministries" and cloak themselves with titles like "brother" and "reverend," but in fact they are merely con men and women who at best occasionally stir up a patient to muster his or her own inner healing energies.

TAPPING YOUR POTENTIAL FOR PSYCHIC SELF-HEALING

Professional healers are by no means the only ones who can help the sick. In fact, many ordinary people also possess psychic healing powers and should use them. In addition to using psychic ability to heal others, it is possible to direct your efforts toward self-healing.

If you wish to heal yourself psychically, you must learn to let go of the outer world so that the inner world may come to the fore and take over, at least temporarily, the functions of life. A broken leg may not be easily healed by psychic energy, but many other ailments can be. In fact, I am convinced that disease is a state of disharmony inflicted on us directly by ourselves or indirectly by others. Even if disharmony is inflicted on us by others, we are to blame for allowing such conditions to persist. Bacteria and viruses certainly exist, but they are always present in the human system. I believe it is possible that these latent disease-causers are impotent as long as the personality maintains a proper physical, mental, and spiritual balance.

If the body's delicate balance is upset by wrong thinking and negative emotions, ranging from fear and anxiety to hatred to destructiveness, from frustration to depression to boredom, then the body must fall ill. Conversely, proper thinking can restore good health. The art of proper thinking, therefore, is nothing less than the key to happiness, health, and success in all spheres of human life. It is therefore vital to learn "proper thinking" to avoid the pitfalls of thought-caused ill health.

Of course, if you break a leg in an accident, it needs to be set and attended to by a surgeon. Thoughts are probably not going to do it. But the majority of all disease—that is, malfunctioning of the body-mind-spirit entity—is caused by destructive thought processes. Once initiated by the mind, these thought impulses travel along the physical nervous sytem and do their damage by causing specific physical reactions and events to take place. Thus, what starts as a thought process becomes a physical illness.

Reversing thought-caused illness is not always easily or quickly accomplished, but it can be done. You should recognize that you have caused the problem, then mentally visualize the symptoms going away and, finally, the accomplished healing. Thoughts, as we know, are electromagnetic impulses—small pieces of energy, created in the mind of a human being. Each thought carries an idea or a visual or auditory image.

Nothing becomes real for us until we think it is real. By themselves, objects, or even other people, have no reality for us. They do not exist as far as we are concerned until we formulate a thought of them. At the same time, anything we can express in thought is *real*, whether it actually exists in the physical, material sense or not.

It is a moot question whether God created humankind in one fell swoop or whether we slowly evolved from lower animals. In either case, humanity is a divine creation, as is all of nature, with its miraculous ways. Even the intricate biochemical processes that have caused life as we know it are a miracle. Attempting to formulate theological truth is not my purpose. I do know, however, that the power in humankind is *thought*, and only thought.

Granted, we cannot all be brilliant, and human personality varies a great deal. Still, I maintain that any normal, reasonably well-balanced human being can influence his or her own life and health by proper thinking. Both illness and healing depend very much on the frame of mind of the person in question—not a state of belief, but of optimism in all matters.

The trick in self-healing, even in a matter as small as a cold, is to suggest to your body that it really can drive out the invaders, function properly, and enjoy the healthy life it is capable of. This power to suggest to your own body, even to parts of your body, *works*. I have seen it work. Verbalizing a problem is no mumbo-jumbo. It is a realistic process that yields tangible results if carried out properly and in a positive state of mind. In other words, doing it while thinking that it might not work is as bad as not doing it at all. You must be honestly convinced that it will work, and work for you it will.

Being aware that we are naturally psychic, and that this gift is present in all of us to some degree, is a first step in the right direction when it comes to healing. Increasingly, we rely on man-made remedies—chemical substances that cause side effects because they are alien to the system—and we seem to have forgotten our mind power. When medical doctors look at illness, they see viruses, bacteria, or toxic substances as the cause. That may be so, but these are secondary causes, not primary ones. The primary causes of illness are negative mental and emotional impulses. We do not usually see them that way, because they please our egos and serve other psychological functions for us. But your basic attitudes—your character, your reactions to the events in your life—are your first line of defense against disease, and that line can be breached very quickly.

What can you do to avoid this? Here we leave the world of physics and medicine behind, and turn to the matter of fundamental philosophy. Too many of us are lacking a spiritual component in our lives. This is not the same thing as religion. Rather, the spiritual way of life is a total orientation toward the positive, in all situations and at all times. This is the way life is supposed to be, and it works.

11

PHYSICAL PHENOMENA— WHEN THE PSYCHIC BECOMES TANGIBLE

ometimes psychic ability turns into something more tangible, more three-dimensional, often in violation of known physical laws. *Physical phenomena* are psychic phenomena that require some bodily action on the part of the individual through whom the phenomenon is made possible.

To understand physical phenomena, it is useful to know the distinction between ESP and psi. These terms were coined in the 1930s by Joseph Rhine (see Chapter 1), and have been in use ever since. ESP refers to the ability to perceive and/or the action of perceiving events or circumstances a person could not otherwise be aware of, for reasons of either distance or time. Psi (short for psychic) is the factor in one's makeup that makes ESP possible.

Mental phenomena are often referred to as ESP and physical phenomenal as psi. In ESP and related phenomena, mental results are obtained by mental efforts, whereas in psi phenomena, physical results are obtained by mental effort. Physical phenomena seem to rely on energies drawn from living bodies, usually the body of a psychic individual and others in the immediate vicinity. The amount of energy required for such manifestations is much greater than that required for the mental phases of being psychic. I doubt very much that psi forces can operate independently of ESP; ESP, on the other hand, can exist without psi. However, if we consider the theory of relativity, which holds that mass and energy are merely different aspects of the same force, the difference between these two classes of phenomena narrows considerably.

Psychokinesis and telekinesis are somewhat overlapping terms for related physical phenomena. Psychokinesis refers to the movement of an object (even a person) caused either experimentally, through mind power, or spontaneously, such as in so-called poltergeist cases. Telekinesis refers more specifically to the ability to move solid objects by the power of the mind. Teleportation is the process or experience of observing such motion. The class of physical phenomena also includes deep-trance mediumship, automatic writing, materialization, and direct voice.

TELEPORTATION

Teleportation is a subject that has fascinated researchers for many years. It usually takes the form of inexplicable disappearances and reappearances (or sometimes total disappearance without reappearance) of physical objects. In the majority of cases on record, there seems to be no rhyme or reason for these phenomena, except perhaps as attention-getters.

Apport is a term used to denote the unexpected appearance or disappearance of a solid object or objects from either a person or a location. There is no doubt in my mind that genuine apports occur, and that the power that makes such movement possible is essentially psi power. Whether the force is directed by an external entity or by part of the unconscious of the individual in question remains a debatable issue.

Some years ago, I had the opportunity to become acquainted with a woman who, it seemed, had a strong inclincation toward physical phenomena. Mrs. M. Ball, a practical nurse with special training in psychiatric work, has experienced a range of psychic phenomena since childhood (she is now close to sixty years old). Teleportation in particular she describes as a "nuisance."

Mrs. Ball awoke from a nap one afternoon to find a greeting card on her chest. It was small in size, with tulips and lilacs on the left side, and contained a Bible verse (Matthew 5:3) printed in Swedish. Mrs. Ball always keeps her house locked—in fact, she has double locks—so no one could have entered her house while she was sleeping. Moreover, even if someone had done so, or if the card had entered the house in some other, ordinary way, it could not have been placed on her chest without her knowing it.

On another occasion, the keys to Mrs. Ball's apartment and to the outside door of her apartment building vanished virtually as she was looking at them. As a result, she could not get back into her apartment, and had to rent a room in a nearby rooming house for the night. Three blocks away from her apartment building, in the rooming house, she dumped out her purse on the bedside table. The contents were few, and the keys were not among them. The purse itself was an inexpensive one, made of plastic with no lining. While it was sitting open on the bedside table, Mrs. Ball had the sudden desire to check it once more. Just as she reached out to touch it, the keys fell to the table with a "klink," obviously out of the air. She did not see them fall, but she heard them.

Once, Mrs. Ball had been working on an article she hoped to sell to a magazine. On Saturday evening, she finished the article and placed it in an envelope, and placed the envelope on the top of her dresser. On Sunday afternoon, she went to make a final inspection of the manuscript in preparation for mailing it early the next day, and found the first four pages missing. She knew that they had been in place the night before. Further, the room was quite uncluttered, and there had been no possibility of anyone entering during the night. Suddenly, two hours later, the four missing pages—together with some photocopies she had not seen for weeks—were lying before her on a table that had been completely bare a moment earlier. They just materialized, face down, on the clean card table.

In these cases, two distinct types of psychic phenomena were actually involved. The movement of the keys and the manuscript were examples of teleportation, which is accomplished by psi power, but the intuition that made Mrs. Ball look in certain places or be near a spot where the missing object would shortly be found was a mental phenomenon, utilizing ESP. Mrs. Ball could never understand why certain objects materialized for her. The one common denominator with all of these apports was the fact that they suddenly appeared out of nowhere.

To be sure, not every mysterious disappearance of an object is due to psychic causes. People do forget or misplace things, or allow themselves to be victimized by others without realizing it. But there have been a sufficient number of cases, such as the ones outlined above, that warrant the conclusion that physical objects can be made to disappear spontaneously and reappear spontaneously in different locations. Why this happens may not always be clear, but the pattern that emerges from these phenomena seems to indicate a dual reason: first, to prove that such phenomena are possible to begin with, and, second, to alert the recipient to a spirit presence that wishes to be acknowledged or communicate.

Psychokinesis, telekinesis, and teleportation are rare phenomena, and generally cannot be learned or done at will. However, there have been some individuals who have displayed such a gift for these phenomena at times. Uri Geller, a medium best known for spoon-bending and colorful behavior, was once walking with a friend in New York City when he suddenly disappeared from his friend's side. He reappeared a moment later, unharmed but puzzled, in the suburban village of Ossining, where Dr. Andrija Puharich, a psychic researcher who spent much time experimenting with Geller, was expecting him a little later.

TRANCE MEDIUMSHIP

There is a human condition commonly called trance mediumship, or, in technical terms, *dissociation of personality*, in which an individual temporarily divorces him- or herself from the physical body, and an exterior or foreign personality uses the medium's body—specifically the medium's speech mechanism—as its own. The medium thus serves as a channel of communication. Serving as a channel in this way is the extent of the medium's involvement in the communication. In fact, one of the earmarks of genuine deep trance is that when the medium returns to full consciousness, he or she has no memory of what happened during the trance, or what passed through his or her entranced lips. In most cases, this temporary displacement of the medium's personality by the outside personality is voluntary, but it can occur involuntarily as well.

There have been some cases in which a living person has used the physical body of a medium to make a communication known, but the largest percentage of authenticated cases of deep-trance mediumship involve communication from a discarnate person (a person no longer living in the physical world) through a living person, the medium. Depending on the exact individual circumstances, such as the background and education of the medium, the test conditions, and supervision of the experiment, information obtained in this manner may be regarded as genuine or not.

The Nature of the Trance State

With genuine trance, the medium knows nothing of what comes through him or her, and does not remember anything afterwards. Trance mediums who are not well trained or who have certain personal inhibitions may sometimes recall parts of the trance material because they do not dissociate completely, but this merely indicates their as-yet-incomplete mediumship. When a personality from the nonphysical world speaks through an entranced medium, the medium's voice changes, his or her facial muscles rearrange themselves, and another person peers out from the medium's eyes. The movements of the hands or body—indeed, the entire personality—are now those of the temporary inhabitant of the medium's body and no longer belong to the medium at all.

Trance states differ in depth. Light trance may be momentary, or a mixture of being aware of being here and yet having someone else work your mind and lips. Partial trance is very common; in that case, some memory remains. Deep trance can be so strong that a person may leave the chair and walk about while under the absolute control of another person.

Trance is not the same thing as hypnosis. Hypnosis is often used to induce a trance state, but it is only a tool that can be used to open the door to the unconscious more effectively or more quickly. In hypnosis, suggestions can be implanted in the subject's unconscious mind by the practitioner conducting the session. Trance is exactly the opposite; here the researcher gets information from the subject.

Demonstrating the Validity of Trance Mediumship

The most important thing in evaluating the legitimacy of trance mediumship is the nature of the material obtained. Whoever operates the speech mechanism and the mind of the medium must be able to substantiate his or her claims and identity, as well as all the facts purported to have occurred in his or her lifetime.

With a trance medium, any researcher worth his or her scientific salt will demand identification of the alleged communicator, and, if the trance medium is genuine, will usually get it fairly quickly, if only in halting sentences. The researcher will then proceed to have a dialogue with the spirit entity, using the trance medium as a kind of telephone, and elicit as much detailed and personal information as he or she is able to, in order to verify it later on. Any purported communicator from the Great Beyond should identify him- or herself in some manner that can be verified—if not by individual name, then by authentic knowledge of the period and place claimed by the communicator. Group sessions are more difficult to manage in this respect. Still, the communicating entity should be questioned as to its identity, and the nature of the material coming through the medium should be examined critically. If the communicator claims to be some vague long-dead "master," the medium should be questioned when he or she is *not* in trance, and the differences (if any) in style, knowledge, background, delivery of phrases, and similar qualities between the medium and the alleged communicator examined. If the medium passes these tests, it can be assumed that the communications are genuine.

I have had a number of occasions to witness genuine instances of trance mediumship.

> Eileen Garrett, a well-known medium, went to a pre-Revolutionary-era house in the Ramapo hills that belonged to a New York newspaper columnist. There she slipped into deep trance and became the vehicle for a badly wounded, suffering soldier of Polish origin who told his terrible story—haltingly and piecemeal, but clearly and in detail, including his name and the names of people he had been with. The authenticity of this voice was incredible; the name and circumstances also checked out.

> Ethel Johnson Myers, one of the finest trance mediums we have ever had in America, fell into deep trance during one of our many sittings. A personality that sounded nothing at all like her spoke through her and greeted a respected astrologer who happened to be present. The two engaged in an hour's worth of technical conversation about the exact positions and orbits of certain planets. After the session, the astrologer went ahead and verified the material given him by the communicator, who had freely given his name, Kamaraya, and the time of his life on earth. All the details, including the entity's name, proved to be correct for the place and time given, something the medium would scarcely have known, as she knew little about science; her training was in music.

From the trance medium's point of view, it is advisable to work in conjunction with, and under the guidance of, a trained researcher or parapsychologist. If a trance medium works alone, or in the presence of amateurs or thrill-seekers, he or she may suffer ill effects ranging from a headache to mental illness, in extreme cases, if the trance is not properly resolved. There are some people who have the faculty of trance mediumship when they do not seek it and at times when they do not want it. They simply slip into trances from time to time, and are terrified at the prospect of doing so at the wrong time. However, this can be controlled by understanding the problem and by firmly applying self-discipline.

Trance mediums are rare. I do not know why this is, except perhaps that the work does seem to be physically strenuous. No one who has worked for many years with trance mediums or other physical mediums can doubt that they undergo extreme stress while working. In addition, it would be virtually impossible for an actor to fake what transpires in deep-trance mediumship in front of the experienced researcher.

The Uses of Trance Mediumship

True deep trance is a genuine psychic phenomenon that can be very useful. In the right hands, it can be very helpful as a tool for scientific inquiry into the nature of humankind. It can also have very practical applications, especially in law enforcment.

> Yolana Lassaw, a clairvoyant and trace medium who often works with police on unsolved crimes, accompanied a New York City police detective to the scene of a grisly murder that had not been solved. In sudden deep trance, the medium—who knew absolutely nothing of the case or where she had been taken—spoke with the voice of the actual victim, and even pointed the finger at one of the suspects.

Finally, trance mediumship can serve as a vital link between our world and the next one.

The human mind—consciousness working through the physical brain while we are in the physical body—is capable of many things that are not acceptable to orthodox science, but that are nevertheless true. Tapping the deeper levels of one's own consciousness, or that of others, and deriving useful information from such sources, is not only possible but common. This is neither supernatural nor in need of being "guru-fied" in order to be valuable, and valid.

AUTOMATIC WRITING

Automatic writing is another phenomenon in which an external source communicates through a living person, but in this case using the written rather than the spoken word. (Automatic communication between two living individuals is possible, but much rarer.) The person attempting to serve as a channel of communication for a discarnate entity holds a pen or pencil and allows it to be guided by that entity. The hand holding the pen or pencil rests lightly on a piece of paper, ready to follow the slightest movement without resistance.

In cases of automatic writing, the handwriting may or may not be recognizable as belonging to someone other than the writer. One thing that can prove an automatic writing to be genuine is recognition of the handwriting as that of another individual. It is, of course, true that handwriting can be imitated, especially if the supposed communicator (the entity sending the message) is or was known to the automatic writer; in such cases, the writer is likely to have some knowledge of the communicator's handwriting, at least on an unconscious level. Nevertheless, graphologists and handwriting experts can usually tell whether a handwriting is a clever copy or the real thing, especially if they have sufficient samples.

In addition to being guided, as it were, by an unseen hand, the automatic writer receives information and impulses to write down sentences faster than he or she ordinarily would be able to do. One of the earmarks of genuine automatic writing is the tremendous speed with which dictation takes place.

The majority of supposedly automatic material can probably be explained as an expression of the unconscious of the writers. However, perhaps 20 percent of such material that has been scientifically evaluated by reputable psychical research societies or parapsychologists seems to indicate a genuine communication with a deceased individual. Proof of genuine communication lies not only in the appearance of the writing and the speed with which the sentences are written, but also in the nature of the information being transmitted. If any of it is known to the writer, either consciously or unconsciously, it should be discounted. If, on the other hand, there are sufficiently detailed and private items of information contained in such scripts, then it is entirely possible that an authentic communication is taking place.

A New York newspaper columnist, who had much psychic ability but was forever cautious about it, was surprised when he received a compelling automatic communication from a man who claimed to have been killed during the Russo-Japanese War of 1905. The man identified himself as a Russian officer and gave his full name and other details that the columnist, with his newspaperman's nose for detail, was able to verify. Why this Russian officer should have picked him to tell his story, however, the columnist had no idea.

Automatic writing is generally done when the writer is alone. In most cases, illegible scribblings are the initial indication that an outside entity is about to possess the hand of the writer. After awhile, the scribbled letters take on the shape of words, although many of the first words transmitted may be meaningless. Eventually, the sentences become more concise and the misspellings disappear—unless, of course, misspelling was part of the character of the communicator.

Automatic writing has its place among genuine psychic communication. If it turns into a crutch a person leans on in order to avoid the realities of physical life, however, it loses its innocent aspects. In some cases, the automatic writer becomes a willing and totally uncritical instrument of the communicator, submerging his or her own personality under the will of the automatic partner, doing that person's bidding, and living only for the next session with the unseen communicator. In other cases, automatic writing is followed by a more sophisticated form of communication, such as seeing apparitions or experiencing auditory phenomena.

In order to be able to do automatic writing—or, rather, to receive automatic writing—you have to have a fair degree of developed psychic ability. It is psychic talent that makes the communication possible, and that is what is at work in this unusual partnership between living and deceased individuals. Finally, there is a certain element of danger in automatic writing. If the automatic writer is a deep-trance medium and is not aware of that particular talent, an unscrupulous entity may use the opening wedge provided by automatic writing to enter the unconscious of the writer and possess him or her.

MATERIALIZATION

There is no aspect of the paranormal that is as controversial as materialization—the appearance of a three-dimensional figure of a dead person that can be touched and photographed, and that acts like a normal human being, at least for a short period. This is made possible by something called ectoplasm, which is used to to form the deceased's "body." Ectoplasm is a waxlike substance drawn from the glands of a medium and closely related to sexual fluids. The British Society for Psychical Research performed a chemical analysis of ectoplasm some years ago and found it to be composed of albumin, a type of protein found naturally in the physical body.

In materialization, the communicating spirit entity—the discarnate person—projects an image of him- or herself on the mental plane, while at the same time, with the help of the medium, drawing enough ectoplasm to clothe this two-dimensional image into a three-dimensional figure. Materialization mediums are a special breed and very rare, and the practice takes a great deal out of them in terms of exhaustion and effort. Energy from others in the room, which should either be totally dark or bathed in red light (under no circumstances must white light be allowed to enter the room), can add to the ectoplasm available for the process. After a few minutes, if a materialization does take place, the ectoplasm must be returned to the medium; otherwise he or she would suffer serious illness due to the loss of so much energy as well as body fluid.

To many people, nothing would be more desirable than having their loved ones once again appear seemingly "in the flesh," even if only briefly and even if that "flesh" is only ectoplasm. But materializations are very difficult to achieve. Consequently, the phenomenon has always been a favorite among fraudulent operators who use impersonators and lights to simulate the process. Unfortunately, if the person seeking the services of such an individual is not too sophisticated about this, the crook is likely to triumph. Serious attempts at materialization are not for amateurs, but should be undertaken only under the supervision of a properly trained academic parapsychologist.

DIRECT VOICE

Direct voice is a phenomenon in which a discarnate entity speaks aloud independently of the vocal apparatus of a medium, producing the sound of a human voice that can, among other things, be recorded on tape. Although the medium's voice is not used, this phenomen nevertheless requires the presence of a strong physical medium. The mechanism by which direct voice occurs is similar to that of materialization, except that in this case a voice box rather than an entire three-dimensional figure is constructed from ectoplasm, and the discarnate entity speaks by means of this. As with materialization, the phenomenon can last only a limited amount of time, and it requires substantial amounts of psychic energy.

EXPLORING YOUR POTENTIAL
FOR PHYSICAL PHENOMENA

Physical phenomena cannot be induced at will, but if you have the gift of physical mediumship, there is at least a chance it might occur if a proper state of expectancy can be produced. To experiment, it is wise to choose a quiet room that is dark or, at the very least, not too brightly lit, and to empty your conscious mind of all extraneous thoughts. Once you have reached a state of mental repose, you might project simple and direct requests for demonstrations from unseen friends on the Other Side of Life.

These are sometimes answered and sometimes not. It helps if you are well rested, in excellent physical health, and not troubled by any problem or extensive worry. However, you should keep in mind that physical mediumship is rare—for every genuine physical medium capable of producing such effects, there are thousands upon thousands of people who are just plain psychic.

12

Psychic Tools

nce the province of gypsy fortunetellers, crystal balls are actually concentration tools that allow a psychic to observe visions. Ouija boards have long been available in toy stores and novelty catalogues, and decks of tarot cards are available in at least fifty different varieties. But how do these tools relate to psychic ability?

CRYSTAL BALLS

The ability to focus one's attention in a narrow channel such as a crystal ball and eventually perceive visual imprints is called *scrying*. Scrying is a talent some individuals possess to the exclusion of all other psychic talents.

How Scrying Works

The proverbial crystal ball, so dear to the heart of the newspaper cartoonist depicting a medium or a fortuneteller, is actually nothing more than a smooth piece of glass (or, in some cases, natural crystal) that captures a beam of light in such a manner that it reduces the outside world to insignificance for the observer who gazes at the light. By thus eliminating external disturbances, the ball allows the scryer to tune in to his or her own unconscious mind and obtain messages from it. Even the colloquial expression, "My crystal ball's a little cloudy," meaning that one cannot see into the future, has a certain basis in fact. If the channels of communication are not open, the crystal will not divulge any information, and the glass remains unimpressed. But we must remember that visions do not actually exist within the crystal or on its glass surface, but are merely reflected by the unconscious mind of the scryer.

Experimenting With Scrying

If you wish to try crystal-ball gazing, or scrying, place your crystal ball on a firm, preferably dark, surface in a quiet room that is not too brightly lit. (Crystal balls are easily obtainable in occult shops.) Rid yourself of as many distractions as possible, and try to put yourself in a receptive mood. Then concentrate your gaze upon the surface of the crystal. Eventually, you may "see" scenes taking place on the crystal's surface. This exercise should be done daily for no more than ten or fifteen minutes at a time (doing it for longer periods may cause eyestrain or headaches). If you are capable of scrying, you should start to obtain results within a week. However, if you readily develop either vertigo or headaches, you should not attempt this.

OUIJA BOARDS

Probably one of the most common questions I am asked is what I think of Ouija (pronounced WEE-ja) boards. More people seem to be using them these days than ever before, and their numbers definitely are far greater than those of tarot decks or crystal balls in use at the present time among occult aficionados.

What a Ouija Board Is

To begin with, a Ouija board is nothing more than a flat piece of wood—whether square, rectangular, or circular—upon which the letters of the alphabet, the numerals one to nine, and the words "yes," "no," and "maybe" have been written.

In conjunction with the board, a pointer device made of plastic or wood is used. The pointer is large enough for the fingertips of two hands to be placed upon it. Some variations of this instrument have a pencil stuck through them. The *planchette* is an older version of the Ouija board that was popular in the late nineteenth century. It too relies upon the movement of a pointer guided by at least one hand.

The term "Ouija" is nothing more than the combination of the words *oui* and *ja*, meaning "yes" in French and German, respectively. The board itself has no special properties whatsoever. Neither has the pointer. The idea behind the Ouija board is that when one or more persons (preferably two) operate the pointer placed upon the board, electromagnetic energies flow from their bodies into the board itself. The energy then produces certain results. These may be simply crackling sounds due to the static electrical energy present. More frequently, the energy moves the pointer about the board. Those who scoff at the idea of psychic communication hold that the pointer is merely moved across the board by the hands of those who operate it. This is quite true—but the impetus for the movement may come from other sources.

The Uses of the Ouija Board

It is my personal conviction that, in the majority of cases, the unconscious mind of the person operating the pointer is responsible for the information obtained from it. This does not make the operation fraudulent by any means, but it does make it, at least potentially, a simple extension tool of natural extrasensory perception. In a small number of cases, however, external entities do seem to work through the hands of those who operate the pointer. The proof lies in the information obtained; if the information is found to be totally alien to the people working the board or to anyone else in the vicinity, and is so precise that it could not be attributed to guesswork or coincidence, yet is independently verified afterward, this constitutes reasonable proof that the information indeed came from some outside source.

Sometimes people with genuine hauntings in their houses attempt to find out what the cause of the phenomenon is. They purchase a Ouija board and try to make contact with the "hung-up" entity in the house. This, however, is not recommended—not because it poses any danger, but simply because a ghost, if genuine, is in no position to correspond rationally in this way, especially as it may be in conflict with the owner of the house.

The Ouija board has also been used widely by people in need of personal guidance, instead of consulting the nearest astrologer or fortuneteller. Again, if answers received through this means could be known to the person asking the questions, or to anyone else present at the time, we must attribute them to the "tapping of the unconscious" of the sitter or sitters. There is nothing wrong with this, and information may be gleaned in this manner that is ordinarily hidden in the person or persons involved. In this way, the board can help unlock deeply felt emotions or information.

But the Ouija board is not a toy. I find the idea of selling this instrument in large quantities to children and young people— to older people as well, for that matter—to be unhealthy and objectionable on several counts. I find it unhealthy because it suggests that communicating with the dead is a game. I find it objectionable because there are occasional incidents involving Ouija boards that are filled with danger. If an operator is capable of deep-trance mediumship but not aware of it, this latent mediumship may very well be triggered if he or she uses a Ouija board. As a result, unwanted entities may enter the individual and take over, and if the person involved is not familiar with techniques for controlling such invasions, all kinds of psychotic states may result.

The wife of a prominent New York publisher used a Ouija board as a lark while on vacation with relatives. More to please her aged aunt and companion than out of any belief that it would really work, she agreed to participate and found herself taken over by an unscrupulous and evil entity. It turned out that she had somehow been contacted by the departed spirit of a murderer who had found an entry wedge into the physical world at that time and place through her mediumship. Because of this careless "parlor game," the poor woman was literally possessed by this and other entities drawn to her, and her involuntary mediumship continued for a long time after.

While occurrences of this kind are a rare possibility, they have nevertheless occurred. Thus, I cannot condone the indiscriminatory advertising of Ouija boards without precautionary instructions, at the very least; in particular, I find it offensive when mentalists—that is to say, stage entertainers—advertise such devices as harmless, when in fact they may not be.

Frequently, unintelligible material or words without meaning come through the Ouija board. Some people have attributed these utterances to so-called elementals, or mentally incompetent spirits. More likely, however, they are attempts by the unconscious of the sitter to express undeveloped ideas. It should be remembered that the unconscious mind is free of all logical constraint and is sometimes quite childish, even immoral, and capable of making things up, even in invented languages.

The Ouija Board as a Psychic Tool

Genuine psychic material is occasionally obtained through the use of the Ouija board, though it would probably occur by other psychic means as well. The board is merely one of several devices that induce a state of consciousness conducive to receiving psychic messages.

At one time, I looked at the Ouija board with a decidedly jaundiced eye. However, I have since had experiences and learned of cases from credible individuals that have caused me to reconsider.

Several years ago I sat with a talented medium (at her insistence) to try our hands at a Ouija board. During that session, a personality manifested itself claiming to be that of a soldier who had parachuted to his death in the Philippines during World War II. He gave us the names of the soldier's parents and the circumstances of his passing. To my surprise, this information proved to be correct. Neither the medium nor I had any knowledge of this person beforehand, and there seemed to be no particular significance for his "coming through" to us except that we had opened a channel of communication for him.

John Steinmeyer, an insurance underwriter who has a strong interest in parapsychology, was working the Ouija board with his wife one night when his cousin Harry dropped by unexpectedly for a visit. They continued with the board, and shortly afterward received a message for Harry from "Fred." They assumed that this would be Harry's stepfather, who had died two years earlier. A third party then began to take notes of what came through the board.

The first four lines were random words without significance, followed by groups of letters, but then the name Jack was repeated several times. Following it came a word that was repeated several times, spelled differently each time—something like "polotic." Then the word "land" was repeated several times, followed by the message, "A land Edith asked about lies between a jambled marsh estate. Jack is crooked. Edith finds a happy life here."

John asked Harry if the message made any sense to him at all. Harry, obviously disturbed, told the group that he had spent the day trying to settle some legal matters relating to property left by his mother, Edith, who had died about six months earlier. The realtor handling the business was named Jack, and his last name, though spelled differently, was pronounced "polotic." Neither John nor his wife, who had been working the Ouija board, had ever heard the name. Also significant to Harry was the fact that his stepfather, Fred, had disliked the real-estate man intensely, and had on more than one occasion accused him of being dishonest.

About a month later Harry went to sign some legal papers connected with the property, and learned that a title search had shown that an estate had once stood on part of the property, which was then covered by marshland. Harry had not known this at the time the Ouija board delivered the message from Fred. Another interesting note is that the spelling in this message was very bad—for instance, the word "asked" was spelled "asced." Harry's stepfather Fred had been a German immigrant who, though an intelligent man, had always had problems with

English—he spoke with a strong accent, often used incorrect grammar, and probably spelled English poorly as well.

On another occasion, John and his wife were working the Ouija board with approximately fifteen persons present, including two young Marines visiting from Parris Island. A message came through for "Bob." Both Marines were named Bob, so John asked for a last name. The board spelled "Bearce." John then asked who the message was from, and the board spelled "Frances." He asked Bob if he knew anyone named Frances and he replied that he did, so John quickly cautioned him not to say anything else that could possibly influence the message. John then asked for the message. It replied: "Be a good boy."

Since this seemed very general, John then asked for some piece of information neither he nor his wife could possibly know. The board spelled out: "escort." This made little sense, so John asked, "Escort where?" The reply: "California." John then asked, "When?" and the reply was: "1955." At this point, Bob began to look shaken. He had never seen a Ouija board in his life, knew nothing about it, and obviously knew that John and his wife knew nothing about what it was saying.

John stopped and asked Bob if he could explain. He had had a dear aunt named Frances, he said, who was now deceased. In 1955, when he was a child, his aunt had escorted him on a trip from California to Pennsylvania. Bob said he had certainly not been thinking about any of this at the time John and his wife got the message.

Now, a very critical observer might think that this material, although entirely correct and personal in nature, could nevertheless have been drawn from Bob's unconscious mind, since he obviously knew of his aunt Frances and the circumstances that were described in the message. However, this would presuppose that a Ouija board can draw upon past memories, no matter how hidden in a person's unconscious mind, and bring them to the surface at will. It would also assume that the sitter's personality could detach part of itself to operate the Ouija board and, as it were, reply to its own questions. All of this is theoretically possible, but not very likely.

It is an axiom of science that if several hypotheses are presented, you should always take the most plausible one. But as long as material obtained through a Ouija board or similar device is known to anyone present in the room, whether consciously or unconsciously—whether of current interest or totally forgotten—a shadow of a doubt will remain. If, for example, one person in the room during a Ouija board session knows a particular piece of information but he or she is not operating the board, this may still be psychic communication, but from one participant to another, not from some outside source. Only if something is communicated through the Ouija board that is totally unknown to all present and that is later checked out and found to be correct, or if a prediction is made that comes true only after the session has ended, can we be completely sure that a genuine communication between a discarnate personality and living people has taken place.

> Mrs. D. Thompson was at a a family gathering when she and her brothers and sisters decided to play with a Ouija board. When the group asked the board where their father had been born, it replied: "Pineyville." They all laughed, because they knew that their father had been born in the town of Doe Run, Missouri. At the time this message was received, the father was not in the house, but when he returned, Mrs. Thompson asked him about it. To her amazement, he became very angry and told her to "put the damn fool thing away." At a family funeral some months later, someone mentioned the incident with the Ouija board, and an elder sister of Mrs. Thompson's father (who had not been present on the first occasion) spoke up, saying that the area had been incorporated into the town of Doe Run shortly after Mrs. Thompson's father was born, but that it had long been called Pineyville by local residents.

In this case, since Mrs. Thompson's father was not present during the Ouija board session when the information about Pineyville came through the board, and since that information was totally unknown to all those present at the time, there remains the inescapable conclusion that this information was communicated to them from an outside source working through the Ouija board, and not from any of the unconscious minds of those present.

Can Drugs Enhance the Psychic Experience?

The question of whether certain drugs can be used as a tool to enhance psychic ability goes back many years, probably to the beginning of time. However, in terms of modern scientific observation, we will limit the question to the past fifty years or so, and to the psychoactive drugs that have been in the most common use during this time.

In the 1970s, British writer Aldous Huxley recommended taking mescaline as a desirable way of opening the door to the unconscious. Other drugs that have been spoken of in this connection include peyote, lysergic acid diethylamide (better known as LSD), and, of course, marijuana. Particularly in the 1960s and 1970s, the field seemed wide open for experimentation with various drugs. Many celebrated mediums experimented with these drugs, under controlled conditions and the supervision of psychiatrists. As yet, the full impact that drug use would have on society had not dawned on us. It was a novelty—something done by the avant-garde and daring—and was said to produce far-out sensations.

As the years went on, the dangers of drug-taking became apparent. Many psychics who had taken even small amounts of LSD in the hope of having extraordinary psychic experiences became ill, and had to discontinue the practice. Some doctors still maintained that only "hard" drugs were habit-forming and damaging to the body and mind, while "softer" drugs such as marijuana were not. Today, though, we know that the results of drug-taking are cumulative and may not show for many years, and there are very few doctors who would consider marijuana anything other than undesirable.

From the point of view of psychic research and my own conviction, drug-taking is utterly useless. Not only does it cause serious disorientation, in the long if not the short run, but the results obtained while under the influence of drugs do not seem to be related to any kind of reality remotely comparable to the realities of genuine ESP experiences. True, the fantasies encountered under the influence of hallucinogenic drugs, especially

LSD, seem to suggest one is entering into a higher realm of consciousness, and visions described by some drug users seem to have the breadth and scope of extraordinary spiritual encounters. But any material gained with the use of drugs is artificial, and is due solely, in my opinion, to the altered chemical state of the observer's bloodstream.

Mental imagery is largely controlled by the delicate chemical balance in the body's systems. When alien substances such as hallucinogenic drugs are injected into the system, they alter this delicate balance and so produce altered states of consciousness. While these altered states may mimic authentic states of bliss or even ecstasy, they are nevertheless due to interference from outside agents rather than to genuine contact with another dimension.

Experimenting With the Ouija Board

Those who wish to use Ouija boards may, of course, do so. However, you should realize that the board may represent a certain degree of danger if you are unfamiliar with the possibilities, especially if you have latent deep-trance mediumship ability but do not realize it. You should also know how to evaluate any information obtained by means of a Ouija board. If any of the information is known to anyone present, it cannot be regarded as true evidence of psychic communication. However, if you obtain material that is unknown to all present and that is subsequently verified, you can take it with a degree of acceptance. In such cases, the Ouija board may very well be serving as an opening wedge for psychic communications.

As for the actual use of the board, remember that the hands of the operators do indeed move the indicator—the pointer— but they supposedly do so under the guidance either of the operators' unconscious minds or of some external source, possibly a spirit personality. It is therefore important to rest your hands as lightly as possible on the instrument, to exert no conscious force whatsoever, and to learn to yield to the impulses received through your nervous system and muscles. It is helpful to clear your mind of all conscious thoughts, to the degree that you are able to do so. Resting your fingertips rather than the entire palm of your hand on the instrument and yielding to even the slightest sense of movement will produce the best results. Under no circumstances should you push or move the indicator consciously or deliberately. This kind of fraud amounts to pure self-delusion, and makes it extremely unlikely you will see any genuine results at all.

TAROT CARDS

A thorough discussion of tarot cards could take volumes, so deep is the symbolic meaning of each and every card in the deck. Originally a medieval device to divine the future, the cards are based upon ancient designs, although there is apparently no record that the ancients actually used tarot cards as such. They were probably in wide use in Europe from the early sixteenth century onward, and they may have been used in the Far East even before then. Basically, the tarot cards contain coded and symbolic information about various aspects of human nature. A person consulting the tarot is, in effect, consulting his or her own unconscious. The cards merely allow you to follow certain guidelines.

How Tarot Cards Are Used

There are various ways to consult the tarot, depending upon the number of cards to be used and the number or extent of readings desired. Best known is the Scottish, or Tree of Life, method, so named because of the origin and appearance of the layout. A professional tarot reader may spend up to an hour laying out various combinations of cards, asking the person for whom he or she is reading to shuffle the cards repeatedly and eventually to draw a set number of cards from the deck at random for the reader to interpret. By touching the deck of cards repeatedly, the person for whom the reading is done gives the reader a great deal of psychometric material (see Chapter 5). In addition, an individual's personal selection of cards may or may not indicate things about his or her fate or karma.

Tarot Cards as a Psychic Tool

More than anything else, it is the psychic power of the reader that permits him or her to speak freely about the subject of the reading, especially if the subject is unknown to the reader. The cards are secondary; they merely serve to open up the floodgates of psychic ability within the reader because he or she believes that they can and is stimulated by the rich symbolism of the cards. I doubt very much that anyone without significant traces of psychic talent can give a satisfactory tarot reading. Countless tarot decks have been sold as toys or as parlor games, but only those who have some psychic ability can use them to advantage.

Offering precise instructions for laying out and interpreting tarot cards is, as mentioned above, a vast subject, and one that is beyond the scope of this book. If you are interested in familiarizing yourself with the use of tarot cards, I recommend that you consult the works on this subject of Edward Waite and/or Eden Gray, which are widely available in bookstores and public libraries.

TEA LEAVES AND COFFEE GROUNDS

Reading tea leaves (or coffee grounds), so dear to the heart of many fortunetellers, is similar to reading tarot cards in that the patterns into which tea leaves organize themselves (or coffee grounds fall) stimulate certain reactions in the psychic reader. A reader may see an image in the dregs, much as a patient may see images in the inkblots used in the Rorschach test, that well-known standby of psychiatrists.

There is nothing supernatural or even remotely psychic in either tea leaves or coffee grounds by themselves. Rather, the result of such readings depends entirely upon the reader, and if he or she derives much psychic stimulation from looking at tea leaves or coffee grounds, chances are he or she will be a satisfactory reader. Of course, if two or more people look at the same set of tea leaves or coffee grounds, they may get entirely different impressions from them because, objectively, the leaves and grounds do not take on the shape of anything pertaining to the future. It is all in the eye of the beholder.

All of the various objects discussed in this chapter can be interesting to experiment with, under the proper conditions, and can promote inner self-knowledge. They can even, sometimes, play a part in genuine psychic communication. However, when they do, they serve merely as concentration points; they have no psychic qualities of their own. It should always be remembered that psychic ability does not depend on any kind of tool or inducer; it is an inherent part of a person's makeup, and it can be enhanced whether or not any such tools are used.

In addition to the items discussed in this chapter, there are a number of other devices now being promoted as being useful for developing psychic ability, such as electrical simulators to "increase psychic ability." In my opinion, these are nothing more than commercial ways of romanticizing a most interesting subject. Other than the ESP test kit now in use at the New York Institute of Technology, where I used to teach parapsychology, or similar kits formerly in use at Duke University, such devices—even sophisticated-looking ones—are of limited, if any, value. These should be treated either as tools to help you get in touch with your unconscious or merely as objects of amusement, rather than as keys to another dimension.

13

ARE YOU PSYCHIC?

Whenever someone comes up with an answer or piece of information that he or she would not normally possess, someone is bound to say, "You must be psychic!" But it is not as simple as that. People can make shrewd guesses, have informed opinions, be experts in a field, or just stumble upon the right answer. But if the knowledge is specific and really detailed, and the person has not had access to that information, psychic ability is most likely the source.

We are all potentially psychic, just as we all have other senses—hearing, sight, taste, touch, and smell. It is all a matter of degree. Just as some people naturally have better vision than most, while others may have more discerning taste buds, so too some seem to be naturally in tune with their psychic abilities. But whatever your degree of natural psychic talent, you can work to make the most of it and sharpen your abilities.

There is no inherent difference between you, if you have natural psychic ability, and a professional person who makes his or her living by using psychic power for the benefit of paying clients. The term *medium* is commonly bandied about in discussions of extrasensory perception, and it is frequently used incorrectly. A medium is a person who serves as an intermediary between the physical world and the nonphysical world, or what Dr. Joseph Rhine, the father of modern parapsychology, called "the world of the mind." *Medium* literally means "go-between" and nothing else.

Many people think of a medium as a charlatan with a strange accent who offers to get your uncle Joe "on the line"—for a fee. Nothing could be further from the truth. To be a medium, one does not have to be an old crone sitting in front of a table with candles, or holding court in the back of a storefront spiritualist church. Any person who has had a number of psychic experiences of any kind is a medium. Based on my experience, I estimate that one person in ten has some degree of this gift; potentially, every one of us has it. It is not anything supernatural or mystical. It is part and parcel of the human personality. Some people are bound to have more ability than others, just as some people are naturally good pianists or painters and others are not.

Anyone who has seen an apparition of a dead person, heard a voice that he or she recognizes as belonging to someone no longer in the physical world, or known events long before they happened, or who can touch a closed envelope and know what is inside—all are mediums of one type or another. Mediums include housewives, teachers, burlesque dancers, laborers, actors, teenage girls, widows, children, grandfathers, Caucasians, African-Americans, Asians, Christians, Jews, Muslims, atheists, and every other kind of person in existence. Wherever the human race lives, there are mediums, and there have been since we learned to walk on two legs.

Whenever someone is able to do something that the ordinary five senses cannot do, we speak of extrasensory perception. This is not the work of the devil, as some claim. It is a natural human ability, to be encouraged but also to be disciplined. By itself, psychic ability is neither good nor bad. If you use it without regard for the limits of time, moral obligations, or physical endurance, it is a talent to be denounced. If you use it to benefit yourself and those who come to you for help, it is a talent to be blessed and appreciated. But at no time is it to be scoffed at or ignored. Indeed, it cannot be ignored.

Most psychic ability is the mental kind—that is, you are fully

Testing Your Psychic Gift

If you wish to determine whether you have basic psychic capabilities, sit in the same room with a group of other people, but at least two or three yards away from them. At a given signal, concentrate lightly on any numeral between one and ten. For about thirty seconds, hold the thought of that numeral in your mind and visualize it being written on a piece of paper at the same time. Close your eyes when you do this. After thirty seconds, open your eyes and look directly at the proposed receiver of your message. Pause for a moment, and then do the same thing with another numeral until you have done it with five different numerals. At the same time, have the intended receiver write down whatever numeral he or she "gets" mentally. You also should write down the sequence of numerals broadcast from mind to mind.

When the experiment is completed, compare notes. Getting two out of five numerals correct is not unusual. Three out of five sometimes occurs, and four out of five is most unusual. The sequence of numerals may be inverted, or numerals may be received out of sequence. This is due to the fact that telepathy works in a dimension in which time and space do not exist, but all things—all thoughts—coexist simultaneously. Trying this with several receivers might be advisable, as people differ in their ability to receive telepathic messages.

The same method can be used to test for psychic capabilities with images, sentences, or visualization of thoughts, except that an entire sentence or visual concept is broadcast. Make the sentences short, though, and the visual concepts fairly simple, as it may be difficult to hold the thought of a very complicated image or a very long sentence in your mind long enough for it to be received. In this case, keep the number of sentences or images to three per session, and record whether they are received completely, partially, or not at all. A 50-percent score would be a good indicator of psychic ability.

Another way to test for psychic ability is to try your hand at psychometry. This is best done on strangers or friends of friends—people you do not know personally. Try touching an object and giving a psychometric reading about the owner of that object (see Chapter 5 for a detailed description of this procedure). Then keep a log of your statements and check in with the subjects of your readings later to see how accurate you turned out to be. If you find that you are accurate about 50 percent of the time or more, you are certainly seriously psychic.

Similarly, if you often—or even occasionally—have hunches or premonitions about people or events, write them down as they occur, so that you can check their validity later—and by all means obey them without question. Fifty percent of "hits" is considered a good indication of some psychic ability. If you do this, you should find yourself becoming more tuned into any premonitory feelings you do have, rather than brushing them aside or suppressing them, as many people do, often without even realizing what they are doing.

Testing yourself for psychic ability, especially if you have not yet had any experiences that would suggest it, can be valuable. However, most people discover their psychic ability through actual incidents in their lives, random happenings that indicate they have the ability to pierce the curtains of time and distance, or to receive information in ways other than the ordinary channels of communication.

What many people call the "supernatural" is no such thing. There are some aspects of human personality and abilities that we do not yet not fully understand, and that need further exploration. But being psychic is natural. Indeed, *not* being psychic is regrettable.

conscious while receiving flashes of psychic insight. This type of mediumship involves the faculties of the medium's mind rather than his or her physical body. Ninety percent of all mediums (whether professional or not) are mental mediums. The other ten percent are so-called physical mediums, whose physical persons are involved in the psychic experience as well. The trance medium is at the top of the ladder here. This is a person able to divorce him- or herself temporarily from the physical body through trance, and lend the body to a spirit or ghost personality to use as it would use its own body if it still had one.

It is possible for ordinary people, who are not in any way professionals, to have deep-trance experiences such as professional trance mediums have. It is also possible to have more than one phase, or type, of the psychic gift.

Evaluating your psychic capabilities can be done in several ways. Basic psychic ability can be tested simply at home with the help of a friend or family member (see Testing Your Psychic Gift on page 161).

In an age of rising intolerance on the part of religions all over the world, foolish accusations are sometimes made by ignorant people as to the nature of the psychic, which they perceive to be "of the devil." But if you believe that we, our lives, are a gift from God, so too must the psychic sense be, since it is a natural, inherent part of our nature.

On the other hand, if you believe that your door to perception is closed shut, then it is. Your attitude is important. Psychic ability comes naturally, if unsought, and in no way represents an evil force. Your psychic ability is your birthright, and developing it depends greatly on your attitude toward it—whether you accept it or reject it—and your use of it. The more you let it happen, the more it will grow.

Reporting Psychic Experiences

I am always interested in receiving reports of genuine psychic experiences, whether spontaneous phenomena or controlled experimental incidents. If you would like to make such a report, you may do so by filling in this form and sending a copy to me in care of the publisher.

Name: _____

Address: _____

_____

_____

Telephone number(s): _____

Age: _____ Sex: _____ Occupation: _____

Place and time of the incident: _____

_____

_____

_____

Nature of the incident: _____

_____

_____

_____

_____

_____

_____

_____

Witnesses to the incident (please give full names, addresses,
telephone numbers, and occupations): _____

_____

_____

_____

_____

_____

_____

_____

Your own interpretation of the incident: _____

_____

_____

_____

_____

_____

_____

_____

INDEX